Rain Towards Morning

Rain Towards Morning

Selected poems and drawings

Robert Gray

PUNCHER & WATTMANN

First published in 2022
by Puncher & Wattmann
PO Box 279
Waratah NSW 2298

info@puncherandwattmann.com

**NATIONAL
LIBRARY**
OF AUSTRALIA

A catalogue entry for this book is available from the National Library of Australia

ISBN   9781922571311

Cover design by David Musgrave

Cover art image © Robert Gray

Printed by Lightning Source International

Author's note

I have felt I could not attempt a definitive book of my poems without at least a small selection of drawings, to indicate their presence behind the poetry. Drawing has been a 'sister' to my writing since adolescence. The free verse line in my poems I see as analogous to the spontaneous line in drawing. This written line is a gesture, also, although for the voice. I have wanted to realize in poetry something like the impact of drawing—the way it is felt directly on the nervous system. The drawings are in a section apart because they are not illustrations.

Contents

from Afterimages (2002)

from Nameless Earth (2006, 2009)

from

Creekwater Journal (1970)

Journey, the North Coast

Next thing, I wake-up in a swaying bunk
as though aboard a clipper
clambering at sea,
and it's the train that booms and cracks,
it tears the wind apart.
The man's gone
who had the bunk below me. I swing out,
close his bed and rattle up the sash—
there's sunlight rotating
off the drab carpet. And the water sways
solidly in its silver bowl, so cold
it joins through my hand.
I see, where I am bowed,
one of those bright crockery days
from so much I recall.
The train's shadow, like a bird's,
flees on the blue and silver paddocks,
over fences that look split from stone,
and banks of fern,
a red bank, full of roots,
over dark creeks, where logs and leaves are fallen,
and blackened tree trunks.
Down these slopes move,
as a nude descends a staircase,
slender white eucalypts;
and now the country bursts open on the sea—
across a calico beach unfurled,
strewn with flakes of light
that make the compartment whirl.
Shuttering shadows. I rise into the mirror
rested. I'll leave my hair

ruffled a bit, stow the book and wash-bag
and city clothes. Everything done, press down the latches
into the case
that for twelve months have been standing out
of a morning, above the wardrobe
in a furnished room.

A Farm Woman Speaks

Winter has arrived, winds scour this place.
Feeding the children broth,
I show them now, through the dull windows,
trees rocked by a cruel cough.

We can't take a bad year,
but the lino looks like an over-ripe banana—
there's no help pacing the floors.
Leaves panic with claws on the verandah,

from trees that boom all day. Usually
you don't notice the noise until night,
but if you wake, you'd swear the sea had come
crashing inland; that awful fright
passes as you realize
where you really are, and where we are
is with crops burnt by frost, the cows
eating dry cornstalks, with all of our care

about three children and a little money
sunken here; with the pasture grass
of a morning, in this worst season for years,
thick with crushed glass—.

Of a morning, I see him let the gates fall open.
The moon thaws. Wind floats bubbles
out of a magpie, and bears upon a salver
the croak of the crows.

He lurches in boots to the shed,
the kerosene tins as buckets drag from his neck.
A fig tree is bulging
its tendons. Fences slop either side, gone slack.

There are still the times when he will turn to me.
I drowse by the persimmons in the log,
and he draws an arm around me.—
Only, those flames can seem then an undefeated flag.

The Kangaroo

His hungry face
moves on the grass, in the way that a final
pencil
will retouch, or the artist erase.

Then, when in flight, the head that was hieratic
is delicate
and remote, before a powerful tight
basketball attack.

At other times, travels with a retinue—it's done
seated, idle
as on a bicycle. (Wheel
and haunch make the same proportion.)

Dogs in pursuit,
he cantilevers on a tail like a tap-root, tears
with stevedore's
hook; while carrying the forepaws of a house pet.

In silhouette, he can almost seem
to make plain
that something unknown
which is able to contain, as one, every extreme.

Morning

I'm stepping around the bare black ground,
wire-netting propped
on lopped poles.
Moss about, bits of brick poking through, and bones.
Rusted wrench
pressed into the earth, jaws open—
the effigy of a lizard. Reeds.

In packing cases, one side gone, the eggs,
in dry grass.
On this cold morning, they're warm, smooth

surprising stone

almost weightless.
Bent over,
at the side of my face the silver
liquid paddocks, and steam.
My eyes and nose are damp, I see through my own smoke.

And I find
a calcific fruit, as if in the pockets of a vine.
Again
I pluck out some warmth of the wintry sun,
ovoid
in the hand.

What is beautiful,
said Ingres, is two colours, ashen or earthen, almost the same,
laid together.

Finding the eggs, the colours of dry sand—

I hold them up
as the boy David would have done
his pebbles from the brook,
taking my time,
to go out armed against the Philistine.

Ten poems

At dusk, scything
under trees by the gate.
The pale moths rise.

The back fence is lifted
in a Hokusai wave,
the morning glory vine.

In the lane, someone
with a scrap of bush,
not glancing up, at dusk.

The ripe days,
the heat, the tenderness;
a white tub filled with green water,
leaves against the glass.

A few cars, way off
across the fields—lost tracer fire
through a bright afternoon.

On this peak, alone—
in the wind, it seems my shirt
is trying to go back.

Sultry night. The moon
small and fuzzy, an aspirin
in a glass of water.

Chopping wood,
I strike about at mosquitoes
with the axe.

In the rock pool, grass
moves with the water. Violin bows
adagio.

Smokestack at dusk—
a woman's long hair
who pauses underwater.

The Hospital

All day I've lain
propped up, suffused
with a book. Dusk

has begun to soak
into the exalted
compounds of the window,

and I settle inside
these cinched, sterilized sheets,
where I am going to be

a while. From one of the other
dimly-lit rafts drifting
through these days

faint sounds of a radio.
A nurse flickers by
out in the corridor, that smarting

vinyl. I can hear
tea trays, coming nearer.
The window is a scaffolding

on monumental
air, and amid that
floats Venus—thistledown,

jonquil. A church bell
has begun, far off,
along the dark clouds,

and children run
below on the grass and
swings are creaking. Only now

does it dawn on me
that this has been
a bright hot day.

Twelve poems

Sanding the floorboards
by hand; in a blank window
hibiscus flowers.

On the enamel dish, slice open
a pear.
Rain hangs in the window gauze.

I get up. Bright moonlight.
The sea is a glass that's brimming
under the tap.

Soaking in a bath.
On a radio somewhere
the time-pips. Three o'clock.

Children's voices,
a piano, in the hollow School of Arts.
In the alley, rain floats.

Long wet verandah,
leaves blown in. Our souls could live
nowhere but the Earth.

Hot night. In the garden,
tighten the tap. It keeps dripping.
The mosquitoes come.

Huge, glittering stars
out among the frogs'
croaking, croaking.

The new moon—
fallen out of its gown,
a white breast.

The rain, soft and everywhere,
becomes cricket calls
crackling, popping in the loam.

In the city
the unexceptional night—
small change.

A drop hung
indoors, from the tap's blunt
beak. A bird sings.

The Meat Works

Most of us worked around the slaughtering, out the back,
where concrete gutters
crawled off heavily, and a fertilizer-thick,
sticky stench of blood
sent flies mad.
I settled for one of the low-paid jobs, making mince,

the furthest end from those bellowing,
sloppy yards. Out there, the pigs' fear
made them mount each other
at the last minute. I stood all day
by a shaking metal box
that had a chute in, and a spout,
snatching steaks from a bin they kept refilling
pushing them through
arm-thick corkscrews, grinding around inside it, meat or not--
chomping, bloody mouth—
using a greasy stick
shaped into a penis.
When I grabbed it the first time
it slipped, slippery as soap, out of my hand,
in the machine
that gnawed it hysterically a few moments
louder and louder, then, shuddering, stopped;
fused every light in the shop.
Too soon to sack me—
it was the first thing I'd done.
For a while, I had to lug gutted pigs
white as swedes
and with straight stick tails
to the ice rooms, hang them by the hooves
on hooks—their dripping
solidified like candle-wax—or pack a long intestine
with sausage meat.
We got meat to take home—
bags of blood;
red plastic with the fat showing through.
We'd wash, then
out on the blue metal
toward town; but after sticking your hands all day

in snail-sheened flesh,
you found, around the nails, there was still blood.
I usually didn't take the meat.
I'd walk home on
the shiny, white-bruising beach, in mauve light,
past the town.
The beach, and those startling, storm-cloud mountains, high
beyond the furthest fibro houses, I'd come
to be with. (The only work
was at this Works.)—My wife
carried her sandals, in the sand and beach grass,
to meet me. I'd scoop up shell-grit
and scrub my hands,
treading about through the icy ledges of the surf,
as she came along. We said that working with meat was like
burning-off the live bush
and fertilizing with rottenness,
for the frail green money.
There was a flaw to the analogy you felt, but one
not looked at then—
the way those pigs were stuck there, clinging to each other.

For the Master, Dōgen Zenji
(1200–1253 AD)

Dōgen came in and sat on the wood platform;
all the people were gathered
like birds on the lake.

After years, home from China,
and he'd brought no scriptures; he showed them
empty hands.

This was in Kyoto,
at someone-else's temple. He said, All that's important
is the ordinary things:

making a fire
to boil the bathwater, pounding rice, pulling weeds
and knocking dirt from their roots,

or pouring tea (those blown scarves,
a moment, more beautiful than the drapery
in paintings by a master).

'It is this world
of the dharmas (the momentary events)
that is the Diamond.'

*

Dōgen received, they say, his first insight
from the old cook of some monastery
in China,

who was on the jetty
where they docked, who had come down
to buy mushrooms

among the rolled-up
straw sails, the fishnets, brocade litters,
and geese in baskets.

High sea-going junk,
shuffling and dipping
like an official.

He could see
an empty shoreline, the pinewood plank of the beach,
the mountains

far off
and dusty. Standing about
with his new smooth skull.

The horses' lumpy hooves clumped on the planks,
they arched their necks
and dipped their heads like swans,

manes blown about
like white threads from off
the falling breakers;

holding up their hooves as though they were tender,
the sea grabbing at
the timber below.

And the two Buddhists in all the shuffle got to bow.
The old man told him,
Up there, that place—

the monastery a cliff-face
in one of the shadowy hills.
My study is cooking;

no, not devotion. No,
no, not your sacred books (meaning Buddhism). And Dōgen,
irate—

he must have thought
who is this old prick, so ignorant
of the Law?

and it must have shown.
Son, I regret
that you haven't caught on

to where it is one discovers
the Original Nature
of the mind and things.

*

'When you see mountains and rivers
you see the Buddha-nature. When you see the Buddha-nature
it is the cheeks of a donkey or the mouth of a horse.'

And he said, Ideas
from reading, from people, from a personal bias,
toss them all out—

'discolourations'.
You shall only discover by looking in
this momentary mind.

And said, 'The world is in ceaseless transformation,
and to meditate
is just awareness, with no

clinging to,
no working on, the mind. Letting thoughts go
as they arise, we are borne on a marvellous emptiness'.

As there's no abiding self
there is no delusion and no realization,
no Buddha and no troubled beings.

Things tells us what we need to do.
Otherwise, we face the wall, cross-legged.
It is nothing but sitting. Not a grain of merit is obtained.

And upon this leaf one shall cross over
the stormy sea,
among the dragon-like waves.

A Labourer

He goes out early, before work, half-asleep,
webs of frost on the grass, wading
wet paspalum to the wood-heap
a bone-smooth axe handle pointing at him. It lifts the block
on a corner of beetled, black
earth. The logs are like rolled roasts,
they tear apart on red-fibred meat. The axe squeaks out.

Raising it
the jammed load pulls backwards,
and now he sinks to where he is. The new tile roofs
encroaching about
in the thin water of the sun;
the lavatories towards here, in the back yards.
Roosters scream
through iron, spurred timber
left stand. Bringing the axe down
bounces gong-blows off the ground, raises the crows;

forging off with rusted cries
into the steam.
He takes an armful of kindling
to drop in the box beside the stove,
and splinters hang
from a red, hieroglyphed hand—
These for the child, who's father to the man,
sitting-up, so reluctantly,
in the small mist of his breakfast.

Nine poems

You forgot the flowers,
I've kept them in a jar.
It smells as if you're here.

I'm getting up later—
these stormy nights of autumn.
Sailboats on the lake.

4 a.m.; the Milky Way
blowing high above the forest.
A truck changes down.

Daytime movie;
and coming outside, it's dark.
I turn another way.

Rainy weather
with the light on all day,
like waiting for someone.

I thought it was rain
and sat up in the dark to listen.
Only falling leaves.

Sunken grave, iron,
come upon, trampling in long grass.
A raindrop slips down.

At lunchtime, the ball
smokes about the grass. A chimney
trails its smoke one way.

The melon, overlooked
out in the muddy paddocks—
It's all right.

North Coast Town

Out beside the highway, first thing in the morning,
nothing much in my pockets but sand
from the beach. A Shell station (with their 'Mens' locked),
a closed hamburger stand.

I washed at a tap down beside the changing sheds,
stepping about on mud. Through the wall,
smell of the vandals' lavatory,
and an automatic chill flushing in the urinal.

Eat a floury apple, and stand about. At this kerb
sand crawls by, and palm fronds here
scrape dryly. Car after car now—it's like a boxer
warming-up with the heavy bag, spitting air.

A car slows and I chase it. Two hoods
going shooting. Tattoos and greasy fifties pompadour.
Rev in High Street, drop their first can.
Plastic pennants on the distilled morning, everywhere;

a dog trotting, and someone hoses down a pavement;
our image flaps in shop fronts; smoking on
past the pink 'Tropicana' motel (stucco with sea shells);
the RSL, like a fancy-dress pharoah; the 'Odeon',

a warehouse picture show. We pass
bulldozed acres; the place is becoming chrome,
tile-facing and plate-glass, they're making California;
pass an Aboriginal, not attempting to hitch, outside town.

from
Grass Script (1978)

Late Ferry

The wooden ferry is leaving now;
I stay to watch
from a balcony, as it goes up onto
the huge, dark harbour,

out beyond a gangling jetty;
the palm tree tops
make the sound of touches
of a brush on the snare drum

in the windy night. It goes beyond
street lights' fluorescence
over dark water, that ceaseless
activity, like chromosomes

uniting and dividing, and out beyond
the tomato stake patch
of the yachts, with their orange
lamps; leaving this tuberous-

shaped bay, for the city,
above the plunge of night. Ahead,
neon redness trembles
down in the water, as if into ice, and

the longer white lights
feel nervously about in the blackness,
towards here, like hands
after the light switch.

The ferry is drawn along
polished marble, to be lost soon
amongst a blizzard of light
swarming below the Bridge,

a Busby Berkeley spectacular
with thousands in frenzied, far-off
choreography, in their silver lame,
the Bridge like a giant prop.

This does seem in a movie theatre;
the boat is small as a moth
wandering through the projector's beam,
seeing it float beneath the city.

I'll lose sight of the ferry soon—
I can find it while it's on darkness,
like tasting honeycomb,
filled as it is with its yellow light.

Pumpkins

What in novels is called 'a grizzled stubble'
on these pumpkin leaves.
The leaves shuffle
as you wade amongst them, their bristles
rustling.
One is slowly stepping upon
egg shells,
pagodas of orange peel,
on heaps of tea slops.
And the pumpkin flower,

a big loud daffodil.
You push about darkness, parting the leaves.
A rooster is on this slope, also;
come to peck
outside, in the late afternoon.
It is putting down its spur
with care
and its eye is flickering about.
The rooster is red
and lacquered as a Chinese box;
a golden hood
down to its shoulders, like a calyx, flexible
upon its body, as it pecks,
flicks,
flicks, and blinks,
pecks. I'm holding one foot up, looking for
somewhere
amid the vine. And find
the pumpkin—
segmented like a peeled mandarin
or leather on the back seat of a thirties tourer.
I break the stem
and lift the heavy, warped pumpkin,
just when the vine's become
too dark.
In between pink and yellow,
its orange tone
can be added easily to the sunset
that's been going on.
I take the pumpkin beneath my arm.
Like a bad painting, this magnificent sunset.

'Smoke of logs…'

Smoke of logs and drifting rain out in the paddocks. Those rolling
paddocks are long grey waves, far at sea, beneath the blowing rain.
And the dark line of bush, a crowd of emigrants at the rail.

Tropical Morning

I wake. The light
is like a divorce photo. And a sharp
bird-note
pierces under the verandah's deep

frontal lobe. Steam
for a sky, where grey rags boil.
The sun, strewn lime.
There re-emerges a cruel

idol, in the cliff-face, over tin
roofs. Dripping, these vast trees hold
a dangle of ganglion.
Dust-churning, loaded with mould,

light burrows indoors, as if
appalled. Each thing is redundant.
This is life
at some further extent.

Another alarm. The alert
sentry, a weapon in its face, was here
in the verandah, avoiding or doing hurt,
and runs away on the bloated air.

Visit

Blown onto the coast road
I go to see my mother, unexpectedly.

Early morning,
wood-smoke in the air. I walk down the same dirt country street

on the edge of town, with duffle-bag,
and find her already in the front yard, at the hose.

She is grey, so grey,
and has her prolapsed stomach. Her hands, lined with garden dirt,

are on backwards,
when they fly to her face and hair.

She must think of something more that I can eat.
On the back step, wintry sunlight gossip.

My brother comes for lunch
and on the quiet he tells me she is not so good.

She does tire suddenly, 'because of the shock', and has to rest.
I wake her last thing,

late in the afternoon. I must be in Brisbane tomorrow,
must catch the bus. Her soft loose skin.

But I'll write. She says that she won't worry
now she has seen me. Reaching up.

I go out to grab a book that I remember I have left here
and find her sleeping again.

Flames and Dangling Wire

On a highway over the marshland.
Off to one side, the smoke of different fires in a row,
like fingers spread and dragged to smudge:
it is a rubbish dump, always burning.

Behind us, the city
driven like stakes into the earth.
Waterbirds lift above this swamp
as the turtles move on the Galapagos shore

We turn off down a gravel road,
approaching the dump. All the air wobbles
in a cheap mirror.
There is fog over the hot sun.

Now the distant buildings are stencilled in the smoke.
And we come to a landscape of tin cans,
of cars like skulls,
that is rolling in its sand-dune shapes.

Amongst these vast grey plastic sheets of heat,
shadowy figures
who seem engaged in identifying the dead—
they are the attendants, in overalls and goggles,

forking over rubbish on the dampened fires.
A sour smoke

is hauled out everywhere,
thin, like rope. And there are others moving—scavengers.

As in hell the devils
might poke about through our souls, after scraps
of appetite
with which to stimulate themselves,

so these figures
seem to come wandering, in despondence, with an eternity
where they can find
some peculiar sensation.

We get out and move about also.
The smell is huge,
blasting the mouth dry:
the tons of rotten newspaper, and great cuds of cloth…

And standing where I see the mirage of the city
I realize I am in the future.
This is how it shall be after men have gone.
It will be made of things that worked.

A labourer hoists an unidentifiable mulch
on his fork, throws it in the flame:
something flaps
like the rag held up in 'The Raft of the Medusa.'

We approach another, through the smoke,
and for a moment he seems that demon with the long barge pole.
It is a man, wiping his eyes.
Someone who worked here would have to weep,

and so we speak. The rims beneath his eyes are wet
as an oyster, and red.
Knowing all that he does about us,
how can he avoid a hatred of men?

Going on, I notice an old radio, that spills
its dangling wire—
and I realize that somewhere the voices it received
are still travelling,

skidding away, riddled, around the arc of the universe;
and with them, the horse-laughs, and the Chopin
which was the sound of the curtains lifting,
one time, to a coast of light.

Seven poems

White rowboat,
slowest wingbeat. A hotel window's
flower-patterned air.

Cold afternoon fields.
The lights of a roadside shop
fill the puddles.

Racing to the surf,
they strike it crookedly
as roots of ginger.

Mountainside dusk;
white flowers through the bush,
the milking-shed lights.

Drying her eyes,
outside on the hilltop street;
hiding in the wind.

The cafeteria
is empty. All the table-tops
in wide morning light.

The torch beam
I feel with through the pouring night
is smoke.

Dharma Vehicle

Occasional voices
in the wind

(Wang Wei)

Camping at a fibro shack
in the national park;
swept with tea tree branches and washed down
with kerosene tins of
tank water.

All the straight trees.
A sea breeze
over the grassy headland, where fallen, white
branches swim.

At night, the splintering of timber on the shore.
Arching above,

outrageous fires.
My bed, a pile of cut fern.

I read beneath the trees all day,
caught up
with those old Chinese
who knew nature is indifferent
and called it "mountains and rivers
without end."

In India, the Buddhists
praised insensibility
to the world
('Doth not the Hindoo
lust after vacuity?')
but with Buddhism's arrival in China,
by the T'ang,
in the time of Hui-neng, the sixth
patriarch, there'd come
a complete reversal of that dharma—
It is not reaching into any deep centre
but to awaken the mind without fixing it anywhere.

'No God, no soul—'
It is all like a mountain river,
travelling very far and very swiftly
not for a moment does it cease to flow
One thing disappears and determines what is arising,
and there is no unchanging substance
through all of this,
nothing to call permanent,
only Change.
That which is the substance of things

abides as nothing
and has nowhere
a nature of its own.
Its essential nature is Nothingness.

I'm woken here when the sun gets to its feet
shouting.
The sun takes a stride
'wearing its waistband of human hair.'
I go out, over the morning's copious small water never touched,
and the golden breath covers the dense forest and the mountains.

Journeys highways railway station nights...

When was it that I
like blown cloud was drawn to follow the coast high road
up and down?

Ma-chu was helped onto the wood platform;
He eased his legs in the Lotus
and laid aside his fan;
he started to trail smoking water on the green tea powder,
beating it with a whisk,
and looked over wet gravel, the heads of all the assembly,
then he said to them, 'There is no Buddhahood for you to attain;
cling to nothing, that is the Tao'.
and signalled for the crack
of the woodblocks together, for them to leave;
and sipped from the bowl, alone.

And there was a master, Hsuan-chien,
told his students, after they'd sat in the courtyard for days,
prostrating themselves, to be taken in,

'Pull on your clothes of a morning
and work along the hillside with the others,
or rake the leaves,
until you hear the dinner drum;
eat your meals
and go to crap when you have to—
That's all.
There is no transmigration to fear, no
Nirvana to achieve.
Just respond to all things
without getting caught—
Don't even hold on to your Non-Seeking as right.
There is no other wisdom to attain.'

Chao-chou abhorred abstractions—
their denial became the whole of his teaching.
He told someone, 'Bring me your mind,
and I will pacify it.'
A nun asked, 'Would you tell me the truth
that has never been spoken?'
Chao-chou replied, 'Look out, the kettle is getting burned!'
He said, 'A blade of grass is as tall
as a sixteen-foot golden Buddha.'
In other words,
'What is there to do in Paradise?'

Dōgen said: 'Impermanence is the Buddha-nature.'

I turn out the lamp.
Leaves, twigs, berries falling
on the tin like rain
in the night.
—It was the monk

Fa Ch'an-ang, in China,
dying,
heard a squirrel screech
out on the moon-wet tiles, and who told them
'It's only this.'

Only this.
A wide flat banana-leaf,
wet green,
unbroken, leaning on
the glass.
The mother-of-pearl of a cloudy dawn.

Brushtail Possum

Thumps the water-tank
from out of a Gothic winter persimmon tree,
ticks like rain
on tin
of the farmhouse
while we're sitting around after tea.

The banana leaves are fringed
as buckskin,
swing in night wind
against a closed window,
the stove crackles
its bone, the lamplight is an olive-oil yellow.

We take some bread out—
a possum hung
over the sag of the guttering,

blackish-grey,
short-ears, snout, anxious stare;
what we offer, it swipes with a human claw.

Eats it there,
nose pink and wet as a tongue,
tightly-packed fur
like moss. One eye is blue-white,
blind
from a twig or fight.

The whiskers are wide-spread like a spider's web.
The face, twitching about,
looks down
with its live eye
as with the one matching the moon,
against the glitter of incisors in a cavernous sky.

Going Back on a Hot Night

Now we are coming again towards a station;
out of the dark
country, the lights of a town,
beyond these sandy flats with their paperbark.

Over a hollow long metal bridge rumbles
the long train,
like a consignment of metal beer barrels
tumbled on concrete. And I see the small moon
above a dark sea, where the moonlight teeters
in saucers, stacked up;

glimpsed as it reaches
to mark the horizon. Now we almost stop;

creak forward. Street-light, palings. Archerville.
I know the Mail—
that I can stretch my legs a while
past these sacks and hampers, along the gravel.

I see a tea-leaf scrub, and the low moon again,
procession of one;
yellow kitchens; smoke; the pond-life of stars.
Through wide paddocks dart, like mice, a few cars.

I stand about. The frogs' hollow, ringing, regular
clonk-clonk, from the scrub—
the sound of a distant hammer
on scaffolding. Going after some labouring job.

Eleven poems

Waking at a station
and across the blue-lit glass
a cold, far galaxy,
the rain.

A flag luxuriates:
the gestures of someone
in their hot bath.

First daylight;
enough for the lacquer to hold
on the dresser top.

Across the level
eucalypt forest, a sunlit
afternoon sea.

Eating watermelon
alone. Seeds taken from
the lips, like hair.

A summer night,
the meandering wake
in waterlilies.

A railway hotel
in the rain. Reading early
by a soapy light.

Struggle to cut
a slice—now the pumpkin brays
like a mule.

In a dark room,
rustle of the long clothing
of the rain.

Hot wind;
on the verandah
a bare rope clothesline
fluttering its hairs.

A milky-grey twilight.
Raindrops on the window,
gulls on the grass.

Scotland, Visitation

North of Glasgow, the train wound like a kite's tail
in the first spring weather,
under a clambering, close horizon—
the skyline, semaphore.
And the brown grass, at the time, with a perfected
bright enamel
for the sky, reminded us of Australia,
of deeply-rolling, open country out from Kyogle—
except for black pine trees
instead of eucalypts
and a sudden tambourine-jangle of light among the beech leaves.
It is a landscape with small visual tradition—
yet the Flemish blue of the lochs, like the Virgin's robe,
and sudden, long hillsides, piebald in broken snow,
brilliant as tropical sand.
Below those hills there were stiff, damp shadows,
pastel rocks, purplish-grey,
the red cattle that are like flood-wrack
hung near stranded water,
and bulging low hills, bound down with stone walls like string.
We passed the upholstered sheep-lawns
reaching to a lawn-like sea,
and grey gables sleeping before a page of the Sound.
And then, neat English cars on the turf,
and the white lacquer and old stone of our ventilated sea town.
I walked all afternoon
on the moor, alone,
with some genetic string plucked and vibrating within.
The only other moving thing,
except for a few sheep, that barely moved,
was the shadow of a hawk

at different places on the grass—
although, in that bright sunlight, I could not find it above.
And just at dusk, there was a lone white bird, urgent
in the distance
along dark water,
before a corroded façade of pine forest.
As though a sword were drawn, coldness in the air.
So I turned back.
The black promontories, spiked and furry with trees,
drifted in the plumed loch.
And it was then I could make out, in the farthest uplands,
dark, brutal-shouldered forms
among a cauldron-smoke… Men have done that
which is done to them. The apparent spirits
in the earth have taught us.
Yet the earth is Empty. It is innocent,
as everything of that replete ground's cruel story
was, in a last consideration, innocent.

The Dusk

A kangaroo is standing up, and dwindling like a plant
with a single bud.
Fur combed into a crest
along the inside length of its body,
a bow-wave
under slanted light, out in the harbour.
And its fine unlined face is held on the cool air;
a face in which you feel
the small thrust-forward teeth lying in the lower jaw,
grass-stained and sharp.

Standing beyond a wire fence, in weeds,
against the bush that is like a wandering smoke.

Mushroom-coloured,
and its white chest, the underside of a growing mushroom,
in the last daylight.

The tail is trailing heavily as a lizard lying concealed.

It turns its head like a mannequin
toward the fibro shack,
and holds its forepaws
as though offering to have them bound.

An old man pauses on a dirt path in his vegetable garden,
where a cabbage moth puppet-leaps and jiggles wildly
in the cooling sunbeams,
the bucket still swinging in his hand.

And the kangaroo settles down, pronged,
then lifts itself
carefully, like a package passed over from both arms—

The now curved-up tail is rocking gently counterweight behind
as it flits hunched
amongst the stumps and scrub, into the dusk.

from
The Skylight (1983)

'In the early hours...'

In the early hours, I come out to lean in the empty corridor of the train, as it's crashing and lurching through the night.

A liquefied dark scrub, and paddocks where silverish-grey mist is rising, slowly as a stirred moon dust.

The orange moon, like a basketball fumbled over waste ground, is bumping among the tops of a dark forest.

In the frosty, thick night a single farmhouse light floats wetly as a flare.

I have lain awake in such a bed, and it has seemed to me, also, it would be sufficient to be one of those carried within this wind-borne sound.

(And I remember the mail train: a fine chain of lights, as I stood in the paddocks of a wintry dusk. Its sound was that of wind through the swamp oaks.)

Travels *en Famille*

She began at once to use the train compartment
as though it were a room at home—
we'd arrived in our hammered, canine furs,
along the platform, through the rain,

and she hung the child's bright socks,
our overcoats and scarves on anything
that seemed a hook. With her best smile
which stayed there, like a transfer.

Two old women, under rugs, were cackling
their uncertainty. The man was cornered

behind a newspaper like a dented visor.
She dried the child's feet on her tartan skirt.

How 'embarrassing'. I could peel open a book…
Schoolgirls, aghast, rubbed off what they wrote
on a glass partition above the women's heads.
The train, given a great kick, began to run

almost at once across an open countryside.
A photograph of assorted river gravel
montaged on one of sodden, moss-bright fields.
Everything creaked like a soldier's gaiters.

The electric light, warm butter; and our coats
stirred thickly about in their steam.
She read out the child's story, and we all laughed.
Beside us, a wall in two equal shades—

the rinsed green of earth and a mauve-grey sky.
A few trees at the fields' edge, as on a shelf,
like old pieces of steel Art Nouveau; their foliage
in the shapes of Japanese fans. I thought

a perfect moment, and forgot about it.
We came to a small, flat town lying in the rain
and through its empty streets a sunset light appeared
shining on the sides of wet wooden houses.

Nine poems

A moon, the last
tilted sauterne, in a glass
that's fire-lit.

The definition
of Art Deco: in black and cream,
a butterfly.

Wintry sunlight;
the plastery legs of a woman
in tennis skirt.

A cathedral—
long tapers of rain lighting
candles on the twilit river.

Wire coat-hangers,
misshapen, in a hotel wardrobe.
Steamy afternoon sun.

On the coast highway
cars blow by in the twilight,
blue thistle flowers.

A late sun
is casting for the fisherman
on the windy river.

Cold swimming pool,
plastic blue. A bare tree,
its roots x-rayed.

Two magpies stepping
on the verandah. Ploughed hillside,
smoke, and cumulus.

A Day at Bellingen

I come rowing back on the mauve creek, and there's a daylight moon
among the shabby trees,
above the scratchy swamp oaks
and through the wrecked houses of the paperbarks;
a half moon
drifting up beside me like a jellyfish.
Now the reflected shapes are fading in the darkened rooms of the water,
and the water becomes, momentarily, white—magnesium burning.
My oars
have paused, held in their hailing
stance—
are melting;
and all the long water is a dove-grey rippled sand.
A dark bird hurries
low in a straight line silently overhead.
The navy-blue air, with faint underlighting,
has a gauze veil hung up within it, or a moist fresh smoke.
I land in the bottom of an empty paddock,
at a dark palisade
of saplings.
Among the ferns, dead leaves, fresh leaves, dry lightning-shaped twigs,
a cold breeze
comes up, rattling in shreds all around.
A wind-blown star
is being drawn forth like a distant note.
The house I am the soul of lies,

hollow, on a ridge across the paddocks, although long occupied already
by the scouts of night.
I drag up the rowboat, its rusty water slopping,
and start off, loosely in boots,
across the spongy, frog-bubbling undulations
of these coarse-bitten flats,
in a sharpened cow-dung smell.
After a day of sitting about,
spent reading and scribbling on margins
or bits of windy paper, and in remembrances,
the hours of which have passed
the way water-drops fill at the downwards tip
of a twig,
I took the rowing boat out.
Rowed miles,
into the river, and downstream, over an ale-coloured brackishness—
through the societies of midges, in their visual uproar
(bronze-lit, like Caesar come to the Forum),
right out, equidistant from shore;
saw the birds swing on long trapezes across the green alcoves;
and followed all the notations of the tree-line
to those at dusk like flaking rust.
I came back with the slow-motion strides of a water-spider over
     fluttered water.
As always, it has worked.
Now the mind is turned down, like a gas flame
in a dark kitchen,
where the wind and all the night sounds can again be heard.
It lies once more beneath the truth of the body.
All of my demanding
has become, crossing these paddocks, and watching the
     other stars appear,
as delicate as the first mould

on black bread, simply to take an axe and go on
   up to the end of the cleared land and under the hooded forest,
to crack some firewood from a weather-tightened grey log,
for a hot, deep bath that I can draw out through the evening.

Bringing the Cattle

All afternoon I've lain about in this illuminated country, on one of the round hillsides, and have heard the squeak of cropped grass, and smelt the cow smell like a warm convalescence, the cows close and oblivious or with a sun-drugged interest.

   A hare stopped in the heat, and shivered, folding back its ears, the same as the butterfly its wings, on a plaited head of grass above the ripe valley.

   But now the farmer, who all year wears shorts and rubber boots, and wades through the running shallows of paddock grass, who cracks his cattle with a stick across their bony out-crops, makes his voice float here.

   And the cows jolt down with everything swinging—the bellies, rounded as hammocks stretched full, and the four long teats, on udders that are grooved and furry like a peach.

   Their foreheads, between the big eyeballs' slow permanent surprise, make a wide, hollow-sounding target for the crowbar-wielding farmer when they've something broken or a germ.

   The hips, draped sharp Henry Moore shapes. And the splayed feet are placed with mincing care, as if they've high heels on.

   Now a last cow is flouncing along the top of the slope, its spider-web fine thread of slobber blown out long in the final brightness of the sun.

   The air is staining quickly with moisture, and the paddocks fill with vacancy.

   There are corridors laid across the beaten grass that are alight and chill. The river, willow-shouldered, that was silk in the distance, now at twilight is all ice panels.

   And the mist that will lie kerosene-blue and thick as smoke, through

the night an incubus on creeks and dams, and will drag among the
raided, fluttering cornstalks, and stick to the turned earth thickly, is
already starting to seep from every dark socket of the ground.

So, following the cattle, and at their pace, I am also going down.

Diptych

I
My mother told me that she had often stayed awake
in those years, and of a certain night
at a rented farm,
on the end of the dark leaf-mulch of a drive,
where she sat in the doorway with mosquito-smoke,
listening for my father, after the pubs had closed, knowing he would
    have to walk
'miles, in his state', or sleep in weeds by the road,
if no-one dropped him at our gate
(since long before this he had driven his own car off a mountain-side
and becoming legend had ridden
on the easily-felled banana palms
of a steep plantation, right to the foot and a kitchen door,
the car reared high, and slipping fast, on a vast
raft of sap-oozing fibre,
from which he'd climbed down, unharmed, his most soberly polite,
had doffed his hat
to a terrified
young woman with her child in arms,
and never driven again).
This other night, my mother was reluctant to go out, poking with a stick
under the lantana, down every slope,
and leave us kids in the house asleep, a cough
trundled among us,

and fell asleep herself; clothed, on the unopened bed,
but leapt upright, sometime later, with the foulest taste—glimpsed
    at once
he was still not home—and rushed out, gagging,
to find that, asleep, she'd bitten off the tail
of a small lizard, dragged through her lips. That bitterness, I used
    to imagine;
she running onto the verandah to spit,
and standing there, spat dry, seeing across the silent, frosty bush
the distant lights of town had died.

And yet my mother never ceased from what philosophers invoke,
from 'extending care',
though she only read the *Women's Weekly*,
and although she could be 'damned impossible' through a few meal-times,
    of course.
That care for things, I see, was her one real companion in those years.
It was as if there were two of her,
a harassed person, and a calm, who saw what needed to be done, and
stepped through her, again.
Her care you could watch reappear like the edge of tidal water
in salt flats, about everything.
It was this made her drive out the neighbour's bull from our garden
    with a broom,
when she saw it trample her seedlings—
back, step by step, she forced it, through the broken fence,
it bellowing and hooking either side sharply at her all the way, and I
six years old on the back steps calling
'Let it have a few old bloody flowers, Mum.'
No. She locked the broom handle straight-armed across its nose
and was pushed right back herself
quickly across the yard. She
ducked behind some tomato stakes,

and beat with the handle, all over that deep hollowness of the muzzle,
poked with the straw at its eyes,
and had her way, drove it out bellowing;
and me, slapping into the steps, the rail, with an ironing cord,
or rushing down there, quelled also,
repelled to the bottom step, barracking. And all,
I saw, for those little flimsy leaves
she fell to at once, small as mouse prints, among the chopped-up loam.

2

Whereas, my father only seemed to care that he would never
    appear a drunkard
while ever his shoes were clean.
A drunkard he defined as someone who had forgotten the mannerisms
of a gentleman. The gentleman, after all, is only known,
only exists, through manner. He himself had the most perfect manners,
of a kind. I can imagine no-one
with a style more easily and coolly precise. With him,
manner had subsumed all of feeling. To brush and dent the hat
which one would raise, or to look about over each of us
and then unfold a napkin
to allow the meal, in that town where probably all of the men
sat to eat of a hot evening without a shirt,
was his dry passion. After all, he was a university man
(although ungraduated), something more rare then.
My father, I see, was hopelessly melancholic—
the position of those wary
small eyes, and thin lips, on the long-boned face
proclaimed the bitterness of every pleasure, except those of form.
He often drank alone
at the RSL club, and had been known to wear a carefully-considered tie
to get drunk in the sandhills, watching the sea.
When he was ill and was at home at night, I would look into his bedroom,

on the end of a gauzed verandah,
from around the door and a little behind him,
and see his frighteningly high-domed skull under the lamp-light, as he read
in a curdle of cigarette smoke.
Light shone through wire mesh onto the packed hydrangea heads,
and on the great ragged mass of insects, like bees over a comb,
    that crawled tethered
and ignored right beside him. He seemed content, at these times,
as though he'd done all he needed
to make a case against himself, and had been forced, objectively, to give up.
He called for his bland ulcer-patient food
and the heap of library books I brought. (My instructions always were:
Nothing by Faulkner;
nothing by New York Jews; nothing by proletarian writers;
nothing by women, except for those shelved under Crime;
nothing spiritual or translated from the Russian.)
And yet, the only time I heard him say that he'd enjoyed anything
was when he spoke of the bush, once. 'Up in those hills,'
he advised me, pointing around, 'when the sun is coming out of the sea,
    standing among
that lifting timber, you can feel at peace.'
I was impressed. He asked me, another time, that when he died
I should take his ashes somewhere, and not put him with the locals,
    in the cemetery.
I went up to one of the places he had named
years earlier, at the time of day he had spoken of, when the half-risen sun
was as strongly spiked as the one
on his infantry badge,
and I scattered him there, utterly reduced at last, among the wet,
    breeze-woven grass.
For all his callousness to my mother, I had long accepted him,
who had shown me the best advice
and left me to myself. And I'd come by then to see that we all

inhabit pathos.
Opening his plastic, brick-sized box that morning,
my pocket-knife slid
sideways and pierced my hand—and so I dug with that one
into his ashes, which I found were like a mauvish-grey marble dust,
and felt I needn't think of anything more to say.

Memories of the Coast

It seemed at times there was no life in the main street of a weekday,
and the road going on dipped beneath the sea,
a wind moving along the water, as though among grass tips,
beyond the flat sheen of the bitumen and the tarry telephone wires.
We kids would come up from the beach onto four o'clock footpath heat—
hobbling barefoot and fast between awnings,
with wet towels, sand-chafing floppy shorts, zinc cream, spiked hair;
three or four of us and dog, counting change,
once more, by the milkbar window's bleached posters, dead flies.
The brick end wall had a Bushell's sign the ultramarine of the sky.
On the way, we passed beneath a paling fence, overhung with paspalum
    heads,
along a pathway of squeaking grey sand,
past a few backyards—their woodpiles, lavatories, long weeds, wide
    underwear—
with off to the side, over vacant land, a railway yard.
We'd come out onto the shopfronts that looked half-witted with their
    sun-in-the-eyes squint.
How poignant, the beautiful, one-handed mannequin.
She was among bolts of cloth as big as papyrus rolls seemed on Sunday-
    school cards.
We went reverently indoors at Papandreou's,
to long floorboards, dusty air, the ice-cream scoops in a jar of milky water,

a dried shark's jaw,
flypaper so thickly used it was like a necklace of apple-pips,
chairs on table-tops,
and a fifty-year-old bristled man who emerged chewing from out the back,
the woman's side of it cut short,
for a fourpenny-ha'penny sale.

At that time, there were only a few fibro weekenders, along the beach road,
among sandhills' fluttered grass,
their water tanks on damp-rotted stands, the flyscreens hung askew,
and a rusty dog-chain stretched toward a puddle.

Behind those places, the low banksia trees' foliage was fused into one
    solid dark clump,
coarse-leafed and sapless;
and when we came out from our games, through that sandy, speckled scrub,
onto blue metal and dust, near the level-crossing,
there'd be a few Aboriginals
going with bottles, on flat pod feet, into the shadow of the railway bridge.

Inland from the train line, the one hotel stood with its high verandah on
    insect legs,
above a bar in uproar. It was there,
of an afternoon, that life was. The pavement
had for us an emollient use, when hosed down, shifting dogs.
In the fifties, most of the larger houses of town were sown loosely along
a first swell of land, beneath the mountains
that moved through every blue tone
of iris bloom, far off within the land's smoulder, a reversed sea-spray.
The dusty streets had mainly wooden bungalows
on low stilts; no kerbs, but each place with its concrete front path,
its silvered steep roofing iron,
and rhubarb in the backyard.

At St John's, there would often be a heifer browsing, Biblically,
just outdoors from the baptismal font;
and inside, someone had told me once, there was a fisherman laid out,
   all his flesh
green-bearded with dangling prawns.
These houses looked over a street of shops and the ply-mill smoke;
the muscle-building
bend of the Coast railway track;
the tiles on the school; a pair of listless rugby goals,
the afternoon drizzle on the ziggurats
of peeled eucalyptus poles;
the Melanesian-looking spindly construction of a long jetty with its crane;
the few gull-molested fishing boats;
and the merchant boat, being slowly trodden down, before it disappeared.
In its estuary, the creek often held an ochre sandbank
of river-pebble shape.
Coming from inland, over a last hill, you saw
all of this, and pinetrees, and a caravan park,
and out onto the ocean, which was too huge to really look at,
in its blaze of whitewash.
All that is changed now, of course, under concrete, car-parks, and a highway;
even the sea, in some places, is blocked out.
We shall sleep no more.
And I am like a salmon that can't forget the place where it was born
and only wants to return there. Nowhere
is like that, any longer.

What I most often remember, of that time,
is just one afternoon. I'd arrived home early from school on my own,
and my mother called me
to bring the washing in.
Clouds were coming up like the Zulu tribes.
And it seemed such a big deal, to be helping your mother, when

she was excited—
she flew down the clothes-line, plucking leaf and flower.
There was a train's whistle
from the shunting yard. I carried everything—
it was bundled into a sheet, and slung across my shoulder.
The first raindrops, blown, I told myself were spears
all around me, as I was jerked about, and bounced, in running
    with my load up the yard.

Some big splattered wounds,
but I made
it onto the verandah. Getting dark in there, behind the trellis,
where leaves were rattled. And she spoiled it all,
by throwing inside a floorcloth and a ragged bathmat and
    running out into battle again
for the peg box—which I'd have done. She came back soaked,
    soaked all over,
in a suddenly smoking rain. No-one could have survived it.
I dropped that game, not to think of such a thing.

Before Dawn

The whole sky, above the wide horizon, is adrift with grazing stars. Then it seems that these are dangled water, and the freshness of the night is breathed from them. In the dim fields nothing stirs, except, beyond a broken line of trees, which are slightly darker stains, a car's light is sometimes travelling. It is quick and soundless, along the far side of the valley, like a goddess who goes running there, while holding up a torch. Soon we will see that she has lit the bushfire of the day.

Curriculum Vitae

1

Once, playing cricket, beneath a toast-dry hill,
I heard the bat crack, but watched a moment longer
a swallow, racing lightly, just above the ground. I was impressed by the way
the bird skimmed, fast as a cricket ball.
It was decided for me, within that instant,
where my interests lay.

2

I remember there were swallows that used to sew together
the bars of a cattle yard.
I would sit in morning sunlight
on the top rail, to feel its polished surface
beneath my hands,
a silvery, weathered log that had the sheen of thistle's flax.

3

A cow was in the stocks with the calm expression of a Quaker;
and my father stretched his fingers,
a pianist seated on a chopping block. He bent his forehead to an instrument
out of Heath Robinson—
a dangling bagpipes, big as a piano,
that was played by tugging on organ stops.
The cow began to loosen its milk: its teats were disgorged,
the size and colour of small carrots,
and milk was flourished in the bucket, two skewer-thin daggers
sharpened on each other underhand.
Then, as the bucket filled, there would be the sound of a tap running

into deep suds at the end of a bath.
Finally, the calf was let in
and that was like a workman building a big lather between his hands.
The concrete in those bails was shattered, but lay together
as though a platform of river stones; and water ran there constantly
from a hose, breaking up and bearing off
the hot lava of cow-pats. That water was delicate and closely-branched
as a long weed fluttering on a breezy morning.

4

There were great dents of cloud-shadow in the blue-forested mountain;
and far off over
the paddocks, through midday heat, the fluttering silk scarf
of a light purple range.
Our mountain was the kite, and those in the distance, its tail,
through all the heat-wavering days.
And many broken, dead trees had been left standing about,
like stone ruins; pillars that held out the remnants
of cloisters and fine stonework,
with rubble beneath them. But the air was so clear, so uncrowded
with any past—
arbitrary corridors, unpeopled, through the air.
Room for the mind to travel on and on.
I used to stop, often, to stand there, in that immense amphitheatre
of silence and light.

5

I remember watching our three or four geese let loose and rushing,
with their heads beating sideways like metronomes,
towards a dam where the mountain-top hung;
and when they entered the water, the mountain's image came apart

suddenly, the way a cabbage falls into coleslaw.
Everything was changed, as easily as that.

6

Since then, I have been, for instance, in Petticoat Lane—pushing by
through narrow, stacked alleys,
among the tons of rotting garbage for sale,
and have seen the really poor.
Those people seemed just dangling paper dolls, threaded onto
a genetic string—
the characters of poverty, starch, lack of sun,
and stunted, hopeless spirit everywhere. Their crossed eyes,
twisted faces, snaggle teeth,
drunkenness were Dickens still, in '70-something,
again in '82.—People in greasy rags, on crutches, weeding wet butts
from the gutters;
spiky-haired, furtive, foul-muttering.
The women were shaped like slapped-together piles of clay. They scrabbled
amongst junk, viciously,
yelling to each other, and oblivious…

What is such an evil, but the continuing effect
of capital's Stalinism?
Enclosure, as John Clare has said, lets not a thing remain.

And then, an hour later, in the West End I found
how much worse I thought the askance,
meringue-coloured, prissy-lipped upper-class face—so sleek
in its obliviousness.
People go rotten with culture, also.

7

Another time, in Washington, when my girlfriend had gone
to see someone,
and while I was sitting at an upstairs window, I watched the bald man
who lived next door, after he'd argued once more
with his wife, come out to stand alone
in their backyard—round as a pebble, in his singlet,
but nowhere near so hard.
He was standing with chin sunk
holding the garden hose—a narrowed stream
he felt around with
closely, like a blind man's cane.
It disturbed me to see him like that—and then, as I started
    to consider myself,
I saw that I was walking
in those silver paddocks, again,
which as a kid I'd known.

8

Or travelling alone in Europe once, and staying in a provincial city,
indolent and homesick of an afternoon,
I turned, as ever, to the museum.
In such a mood, however, the masterpiece will often no longer serve:
it seems too strenuous and too elevated;
it belongs in a world too far beyond one's own.

From experience, one has learned to follow at these times
    that arrow, *Ecole francaise*
XIXme siècle. There, on an attic floor,
unnoticed by the attendant, a newspaper crumpled
over his boots, or along the deserted outer corridors,

beneath tall windows, in the light from which
many of them are cancelled,
hang one's faithful mediocrities—in sympathy with whom
one had thought to be borne through until dinnertime.
Armand Guillaumin, Léon Cogniet, Jules Dupré, Félix Ziem:
no artistic claims can be made for these. Their sluggish or
    bituminous pigment,
greasy sheen, and craquelure,
their failures, so complex and sad, have earned them
'an undisturbed repose'.
And yet, even these harmless,
unassuming and forgotten, as I glanced among them, on this occasion,
were forgotten
by their one idle, arbitrary re-creator,
and the landscapes that came far more vividly before my eyes
were all memories.

9

Into my mind there has always come, when travelling,
images of the twisted Hawkesbury bush
crackling in the heat, and scattering its bark and twigs about,
white sunlight flicked
thickly on the frothy surges
and troughs of its greenery; and within those forests,
great pools of deep fern, afloat
beneath a sandstone rock-lip; and of the Platonic blueness
of the sky; and recollections of Coledale and Thirroul
on their clifftops, where sea-spray
blows among the pines and eucalypts; and, most of all, of those forests,
cool, light-flouncing, with white female limbs,
and the yeasted green pastures,
where my mind first opened, like a bubble distended from a

glass-blower's tube,
and shone, reflecting
things as they are—
there, where I have felt, anxiously, I would find them a while longer,
after passing Kempsey, once more, on the mail train of an early morning.

from
Piano (1988)

Black Landscape

All of the high country, that year, had been burned-out
with the headline blackness of war.
Soon afterwards we came travelling through the place,
along a ridge's blade-edge by car.

The tree-forms then were the crudest of hieroglyphs—
a crushed charcoal scrawl;
petrified in their extreme gestures, about those hills
steep as a landslide sprawl.

Rain-storms had just been there: in overcast light
boulders exuded shine,
and the clinkered valleys were backed with high, wet cliffs.
An immense open-cut coal mine.

We were creeping through winds that pounded on the car,
twanged it, made it a cripple,
that seemed to compress its shape. But stopped to photograph,
the car braced like a mule.

Climbed down, into stillness and deadness. The clay slopes'
squirming runnels, closely traced,
left earth hung between horizontal strata—a Hindu façade,
now almost effaced.

A crow blew away, with a shout; I thought of having to eat
such dry fibre. Keats didn't know
all about those syllables, 'forlorn', who'd never heard
a sound like the bushfire's crow.

Everywhere, great ruptured webs, the shining charcoal bushes.
Twigs traced and smudged us black.
I saw ahead, in profile, how a cliff-face was built of shale:
the silverfishes' newspaper stack.

Smell of wet ashes, and trickling water. We found
headless trees breaking there
into fine leaf again: their boles were stockinged with them
as with flame. A tremulous mohair.

In red and green of an apple. So: fire, air, water, earth;
each contending with another;
shifting of energies, as animals shove in their sleep. And life,
too, where things are sore.

I took from beneath a stone the cicada: six-legged tottering,
three clear jewels on its brow,
a samurai's orange mask. Those beautiful gauze wings
segmented with a gum tree bough.

Between such branches, if you tilt your hand, you can make
a light, pale blue and frail
as after sunset. I told a girl once, in Ireland, of cicadas;
she said, 'We only ever had a snail.'

Very Early

Birds are drifting, bubbles on the eyesight, in a frangipani sunrise.
Waves nod as a rocking horse would
if before French windows it stood
and stirred with the air, On the bay lies
a diamond flotilla. And right the length of the harbour
a light stretches: one duellist and the other.

Or it's the weavings of an immediate Penelope. Now, the trunk of light
is speckled about with leaf-shimmer.
On many a verandah
the summer mist of the mosquito net
is still abroad: the hypotenuse at ease.
Curlicues on a dog's back are being planed by the breeze.

The dog, tongue loose as a pocket hanging out,
is leaving the reserve (these roman candles of green,
the lawns pebbly with dew, and moored yachts with their bathroom sheen);
it blows away into the open barn door of a street,
dimly complacent, following some hunch;
a small, dark bird in there shifts like a sparkle on a branch.

Here at the park, a turbaned snail, the potentate of the dew,
majestically moves. Gum leaves are eyebrows being
drawn on pallor. A spider's hung in the midst of dawn.
The pine trees, at a distance, seem water stains down a plastery blue.
If no-one saw all this, it would go on just as well,
but there is here what only words can tell.

Byron Bay: Winter

Barely contained by the eyesight,
the beach makes one great arc.
There overlap behind it
blue ranges, each a tide-mark.

Beside me, swamp-oak's foliage
streams, with the looseness of rain.
Out in the heath, a guard's carriage
follows the vats of a train.

Beyond, cloudy afternoon swells,
the purple of claret stain.
The sunlit town's strewn like petals;
its lighthouse, a tiny pawn.

When far off, I turn. The sun brings,
because of its perfect warmth,
the feeling you could wear great wings
while stepping along the earth.

Harbour Dusk

She and I came wandering there through an empty park,
and we laid our hands on a stone parapet's
fading life. Before us, across the oily, aubergine dark
of the harbour, we could make out yachts—

beneath an overcast sky, that was mauve underlit,
against a far shore of dark, crumbling bush.
Part of the city, to our left, was fruit shop bright.
After the summer day, a huge, moist hush.

The yachts were far across their empty fields of water.
One, at times, was gently rested like a quill.
They seemed to whisper, slipping amongst each other,
always hovering, as though resolve were ill.

Away off, through the strung Bridge, a sky of mulberry
and orange chiffon. Mauve-grey, each cloven sail—
like nursing sisters, in a deep corridor: some melancholy;
or nuns, going to an evening confessional.

Walking Around at Night

The rising moon appears,
softly focused as a movie queen,
in a close frame
through the kitchen flyscreen.

I stroll outside and down the path,
leaving a radio;
the moon is buxom
behind the curtains of the willow.

It's soon an old fumy paraffin lamp
of a moon, that I prefer.
The hammer blows of barking,
a car clearing its chest, somewhere,

the slam of a tinny garage door
on concrete, and the voices
going inside that could be either
quarrelsome or boisterous.

I keep walking. A cow and the moon
(it's white as salt now), each a term
in some kind of sequence. I shoo
the cow, for a place to lie that's warm,

under a lichen-smoke and bird'segg sky.
Adrift on the rising night.
Going on, toward a razor-strop highway;
its streaks of light

are suddenly lifted away at the curve
and gone, each a stroke;
and the occasional heavy flat backwards
stropping, of a truck.

Waiting to cross (a short-cut back), I stand
in weeds. At every car,
they're strung with glutinous, distended drops.
The moon is bright as an old scar.

Prunus Nigra

The plum tree with popcorn blossom
is pink upon the frost,
or it's embossed on the dusty blueness
of the lower sky, toward dusk.

A magpie, ragged witch-doctor,
long-jumps to the clothes-line pole;
behind it, the plum tree bursts
like a wave at sunset.

How terrible it would be
if this plum bloomed near the palings
and you saw it with the memories
of some other life.

Fire Sermon

The lissome bay is silvered slightly, in its supine lightness;
a stocking-textured water
takes the morning's cerise.

But soon, between the headlands, sea and sky are solid blues
that have closed, almost
seamlessly, like stone.

And yachts have come out to climb on the sea's face, slow
and wavering—the way
that cabbage moths walk.

These foreshores are deeply tented in eucalyptus saplings
and tea-trees, leaned
on the engorged light.

Here cicadas' sizzling strapped toffee strings of sound,
filmy and flashing, fuse
into sheets, all around.

Now the rhythmical light-points shoal the water thickly
as the shift to shovelled
gravel in cicadas' song.

Simmered eucalyptus oil vaporously uncoils, accompanying
angophoras, the dancing
Indras of rosy stone.

Dilated summer. It seems you can see into the Flame, while
light-cells teem, cicadas thrum,
to its naked sensuous events.

On the far shore, house-faces are hung, white muslin among
bush humble as rubble
in the blue Empire.

I have left everything behind, for an endpaper shore; to lie
under membranous layers, as
lights vault, coagulate, rebound—

to see one ignite another, billowing, and genealogies decline;
to watch here day's ardour
that turns water into wine.

Sixteen poems from the Japanese

Even now, I never linger
by this valley stream,
in case my shadow
flows back into the world.

> —Dōgen

Ah, how many dewdrops are falling
from the stems of grass,
now that the autumn winds have come
to the fields of Miyagino?

> —Saigyo

Sorcerer, who flies through heaven,
find for me the one
who has never yet appeared,
not even in my dreams.

> —Murasaki

In the shade of a willow
by the road
the clear water is running.
I meant to pause here
only a moment.

—Saigyo

Water drips from moss
among the mountain stones,
and I am rendered clear.

—Ryokan

The days that have gone by
leave one sad,
and yet they were all of them
only a dream.

—Former Emperor Hanazono

I sit and look back on
days that have gone.
Did I dream them all,
am I dreaming now?
Listening to winter rain.

—Ryokan

A light snowfall
and within that
a billion worlds arise
and within that
a light snowfall.

—Ryokan

Haze rises
at the end of a spring day
that I have spent with children
bouncing ball.

—Ryokan

As the sunset ends
and the mountains are hidden,
further off
other mountains appear.

—Kyoguku Tamekame

In my home town
the cherries are in bloom
and spring is passing by
the same as ever.

—Dōgen

Early summer rain
has left in the roadway
a hall of light.

—Basho

Ah, look!
The mushroom-gatherers missed
five dewdrops.

—Buson

A camellia fell;
the monk smiled
going by.

—Hori Bakusui

Clear autumn day;
my wife doesn't even notice
we pass each other.

　　　　　　　—Nishigaki Shu

The crows' calling
ends.
Twilight snow.

　　　　　　　—Aro Usuda

Translated with Kazuaki Tanahashi; Zen Centre, San Francisco, 1982

The Shark

There are tons of the sea's loose flesh above, made to jostle
and shimmy,
an immense, shadow-tainted
clear jelly.

It shoulders and displaces itself about itself,
on the peaked and scooped plain,
harried like migrant reindeer,
lava-bright or wind-torn.

The diver goes on steadily sinking, spread on shadow
as if to drown;
weighted, he feels ducked and
pole-pressured down;

only his breath seems to panic, and he turns to watch it pass,
wobbling and clinking upwards

into light:
a stairwell that the mind climbs and breaks like glass.

The long sunlight sways here
in columns, as though a bundle of lift cables.
With its withered Red Indian head
a turtle's

struggling up steeply
on stumpy wings—an ennui, bound in horn,
a broken beak.
Bevies of fish are making little mouths to squeak

like society girls, in their spotted or banded
wafting chiffon,
and with impenetrable dead eyes. The jelly fish,
a huge heap of frog spawn.

Something stares sideways
that has Caligula's profile, and the teeth of an offender
in chrome. As a spinning hoop
when it's coming to rest surrounds a

centre, touching all parts of the rim,
so in leathern skirt the rat-tailed
manta ray, flapping,
is hung in the grit it's flailed.

The shark comes drifting with silent engine
through water thick as smoke,
a space craft called on by a distant gravity,
out of the murk.

It can loosely swathe
a limber grey fuselage.
It moves with all the potential and ease of someone
turning out of a garage.

The long body wavers beautifully
and easily,
as a train at dusk
through the curves in the floor of a valley.

The gills, for all their deepness,
are each neat
as a Japanese slit;
the head's simply rounded-off and incorporate

like the nose of a surfboard—it is not the authority
for anything within;
the head, amid jungle light, seems less important
than its fin.

It has the senile, yellow, ill-wishing look
of a hillbilly grandma's
uncomprehending eyes, and what seems her mouth
in its Greek mask melancholy or tooth-stump uncouth—.

But a foolish guffaw
and that vacuousness is filled with doubled barbed wire
or, closer,
a wreath, with each leaf a razor.

The mouth is a picket of backward serrations;
the skin, sliding ground glass.

The diver waits with his single fang poised, for the tonnage
of its flick-pass—

imagining the voluptuous greedy wriggle
of its packed dog's body
and himself clamped too overwhelmingly, too rigid,
for struggle.

This energy, this pure appetite, that's
prior to the mind, this
is the thriving pathology
which is life; here elegant, as though wriggled from a thesis.

The effort to overcome it, in art, love, religion,
remains that devious will.
Nothing can be done about such greed, except to observe it
in hopelessness, which makes us still.

To Philip Hodgins

I sit in an empty restaurant, at a table with a view
through plateglass, onto tree-tops growing dark.
The sky is a new carbon paper's deep, remote blue;
the lamps, skimmed ocean moonlight, through the park.

Foliage near those lamps looks chipped as woodcuts;
and buildings the shape of cabinets, beyond there,
are left open on digital batons—their neon lights
arrayed with all the warmth of a questionnaire.

Midway and dark mauve, the stone of cenotaph
in Art Deco style, with soldiers that are shades,

along its highest ledge: they're led to by every path,
hunched in greatcoats, helmeted. This pervades

the restaurant's image, now hung outdoors. My cloth's
whiteness, glasses, silver, in their projection,
make a dais before it. And the napkins, tall, grave yachts,
range far off, under strung planets' conjunction.

Our light is being proffered, rococo, unfunctional,
to the nearest stone conscript, who could seem,
beyond that insubstantial, glittering, decorous table,
someone brittle as salt in a waiting room.

The mausoleum has the presence of Böcklin's 'Isle
of the Dead.' Yet leaves are blown aside, people walk
unperturbed, within a sea so dark and mobile;
and Philip arrives with books and poems, and we talk.

Description of a Walk

In the shape of long sand-dunes, but apple green,
the pastures I'd crossed. A quiver of rain
hung above them. One currawong somewhere, warbling
happily as a hose within a drain.

The forest was cumulus on stilts, from afar;
everywhere inside it, leaf-splatterings and spar;
the leaves, paint clots, or a fringe of trickling.
Angry as a burned insect, a distant car.

The forest closed. I climbed among sandstone—
great gouts of lava, petrified as iron;

puffed like fungi, or with a broken iceberg's edge;
all of a rusty red or burnt orange tone.

About the plinths and mantels was an artful
pebble-scatter; on its pedestal, an eccentric bowl.
Rose-coloured sandstone syncopated salt.
Blown rain was being emptied by the bushel.

Uphill, warped arcades of bush, rack on rack;
reiterative as cuneiforms. Bacon redness of bark,
or smooth wet trunks of caterpillar green,
and some with a close dog's fur, greyish black.

Other colours: Brazil nut kernel, an unfired pot.
In the wet, tart as bush smoke, a sweet rot.
The air rain-threaded, as though with insect sounds.
My heart flapped like a lizard's, by the top.

Underneath a clay bank, an old grey gutter,
now sealed with smoked glass. A claw of water
flexed nearby, on rock ledges and over roots—
a wide-toothed, vibrating cane-rake's clatter.

Sprigged trees; a vista of Pre-Raphaelite shine:
beneath gentian hills, a billiard table green;
ploughed land, pumpernickel; the road, a fracture;
the shapes of coral in a dark tree-line.

Rain shaded to silence. Then cicadas' shekel
sound.—Emptied from a bucket, a pile of shell
poured with the numerous headlong pour of sand
onto other shells. A dry calcite rattle.

This merely the start—the warming of an engine.
Each opens a row of gills; if you find one
you see almost through the body. Their joined hum's
power, an electricity substation.

I walked on and on, in such vibrance. Wet light
gave the leaves' undersides a tinfoil glint.
Rag and bone bushland. White arms lifted, dangling
cloth. That chant. What it was all for I forgot.

A Winter Morning

For a few minutes more now all the day's furniture
will remain sheeted in a shuttered room.
With the convalescent gleam of barley sugar
the lights along the by-pass are still drooping in bloom.
Here, two headlights on a lane,
easing downstairs. In wood and fibro, my cathedral town—
such this valley. *Materia* is mater; substance is womb.

I go along backyard fences through some fog—
most are patched with old corrugated iron—
onto a plumed, translating hillslope, with someone's dog;
high up, the sky is lifting, become woodgrain:
its whorls, dabs, darts, long streaks of golden cloud,
on airiest blue. The weeds' strung fruits wear a globed
insect's opal glitter. A dank tree-line,

where eucalyptus are the blue of husky voices;
their elevations, declivities all have accents
flying. I'm here alone on a Sunday, for the offices
of matter—poinsettias, more red than sacraments;

a sceptred palm-tree's golden smoulder; this insouciance
of levitated pink; the frost's lime effulgence...
It is the same lesson: ease of their relinquishments.

A Summer Evening

They still do as was always done:
they call the children just on night
then make sure of the fly-screen catch,
while moths knock down a shaggy pinch
off themselves or the porch light.

And insects race their bobbins, thick
as a sweat shop, as grass itch,
as matted grass seeds that are stuck
smudgily in bleached leg-hairs.
Another sound: a nutmeg-grater scratch.

It is the time of 'Look at yourselves!'
One who's not a parent gazes out
at tree-shapes spread like peacocks on
a lake (the town); at grass-loop shine;
at the lighted façade of this street.

And likes the way the paling fence below
is reclining into weeds. A thickened tree
by the house has its bole brush-swiped
with shadow. At this time the milkman came.
Now, the marching-girl movements of TV.

Another way, a neon sign, and trees
rank as weeds; and the last, squeezed light,

beautiful and calm—as when illness cleared
her face. And you had thought, Why not
like this always? Why now, too late?

Nine Bowls of Water

Clear water, in silvery tin dishes
dented as ping pong balls:
a lemon juice tinge of the staling light is in them;
they've a faint lid of dust.

A potted water along a board, slopped
and dripping lightly.
While the men work on the city road, excavating
its charred blackness,

the water waits
behind a corrugated iron shed that is set
at the pavement front,
under the tall shadowing empty stadium.

On that low plank, also, crude soap pieces,
bright as the fat
of gutted chickens—but, with a closer look, resistant,
darkly-cracked, like old bone handles.

One beside each bowl;
and the rags are on their bits of hooked wire.
The cars continue,
but few people walk here between the lunch shed

and brick wall. Set out along a wet bench,
the kneeling water,
from which we have dreamed the spirit.
We walk in grittiness,

on papers, plastic scraps, mud-scrapings,
splattered with a sporadic jackhammer racket,
past nine bowls of water, a gallantry of the union.
Trees in avenues and sailing boats and women.

from
Certain Things (1993)

Currawongs

Dinner-jacketed, these mafia stroll on the park to air
a respectability.
Our acquaintance long made, it seems assumed we couldn't care
they have no morality.

They've brought the peeled-looking nestlings to eat on our clothes wire,
where we had offered them bread;
have often chosen to chuck down here the cellophane wrapper
and the moulded plastic head

of cicadas. One slowly ate a silhouetted grasshopper,
lifting it in a fanfare,
stylised with pride, as though it were holding a broken swastika.
They have tightly brushed-back hair,

snipy Latin features, an expression like a thin moustache,
but the eye is demonized
and belongs to an African carving, more than to an apache.
The eye, barely capsulised

in its split pod, has a rind of poisonous yellow around
its blackly shining, opaque
pupil. It is watching every movement in the air, on the ground,
as if it were a card-stake.

These birds live more intensely than any gangsters on the run.
Although, at times they'll deploy
with police cars' confidence—another role they have taken on—
sounding their *calloy, calloy,*

calloy, a siren, ordering the neighbourhood. On the grass
they appear to strut with arms
slightly akimbo, and with the sense of limited nimbleness,
the stumpiness, and what seems

the tilted head, alert for notice, of a bodybuilder.
And then, the pin-pointing beak
is applied quickly, intently, while staring like a welder.
I noticed one had grown weak,

in the park, below the railing. Through a bright afternoon
it stood drowsily about,
although wary, and when at last the darkness had sifted down
it was killed, by leaping out,

suddenly, under the only headlights in some while on our street,
confused, at the last minute.
That most resonant thump, of something live; and also, I thought,
crunch of bird-twigs. I found it

still breathing, horribly; the beak split wide, and held by a thread,
as when firewood is splayed,
the eyes squeezed hard, without lashes or tears. It lay crash-landed,
crumpled. I ran for a spade;

and answered, 'Don't come,' disentangling the blade in the dark;
came back, to find it gone—
and saw two boys, holding something on the far side of the park,
who looked behind as they ran.

God no, I thought, they'll poke about, then toss it into a lane,
soon bored, or over a fence

to a dog, and cackle and run on, already with some new plan...
Those birds are their most intense

at twilight, in scalloped flight, against the horizon's fire-coal
orange, where it tilts a ramp
onto indigo. They strictly show and close the wing's porthole
like a signalman his lamp.

There are some admire them, who admire what remains of them in us,
who admire the deed, elan,
health, affirmation; but now what I see, also, is the pathos
of braggarts and the strong.

At dusk, among the drawn latex strands of vast grey fig trees,
the currawongs' wild yodels,
scored through the harbour—the waves have sails like beer-bellies—
listless as rubber sandals.

In Thin Air
for Dee

It's songs of you that they play
while I eat alone
the grease of one more café
in an overnight town;

but the arrangements are made,
the paperwork's done,
and the money has been paid,
so I'm going on.

I'll have to go much further before
turning home.
There's kindness of a stranger;
the best is long known.

Icicles, knobbly as candlewax
that's long on bottles
or hung from candlesticks,
along the hotel lintels,

where I say your name to ingots
in purple night; to steam
above a few houses; to overcoats,
women inside, blown home.

The snow is shapely as meringue,
thousands of miles to come—
I have done such things too long.
Tips of obelisks in foam,

as we came by, were cemeteries;
a river, grey-veined marble;
the mauve, stiff-frozen smoke of trees;
snow smothering every gable.

A corruption is waiting hidden,
Conrad somewhere said,
even for affection so freely given
as ours; much is paid.

I lie in the long midnight train.
Thickly, black pinions fly;

we howl through a forest like wolverine.
Dawn's weird chemical sky.

Most of the day, keeping on
through Canada, I forget
the book I am reading, well begun,
because of looking out—

to wet black trees, snow-sprayed
one side (as if arc-lamp
lit), all of them fraying, then frayed;
to lakes, cold fat on soup;

to a young woman, in the snow
and steam we'd driven,
standing at nightfall to see us go
at a forest stop, on her own.

Plain houses, of doors and windows;
calcified silos, stables.
Out here, occasional light shows,
early, and warm as waffles.

In the Rockies, one's enthusiastic:
sunsets built of stone.
I thought of that haiku, 'A firefly, look!
Forgetting I was alone.'

There was a waterfall at full stint,
frozen to its rock,
like quartz or a stroke of paint.
We've stopped again. Taking stock,

it seems that I've gone far enough
to be offered normal life,
as though flipping over a disc.
I'd never thought to ask.

My life, I imagined, must be a hymn
to the optic nerve.
Other senses, you have proved,
will have all they deserve.

A Testimony

Gloomy midnight in spring, rain sinking on the canes in the garden.
I wanted some ease to my confusion, and reached out through
    lamplight for a pen.

I am one of those who have watched their image in the hearth, where a
    fire was tearing itself to pieces, with its nails and with its fists.

And when shall I lie again in a landscape that is bright like satin
with my Venus of the sweet grass, her breasts as plump as quail?

Shall we sing hymn three-six-six: 'Art thou weary, art thou sad?' As
    though it matters,
for who are we? Blowing in the abyss, these crying-out shapes of smoke.

The one perfection of the world is lust: is grasping, scheming, longing.
    And entirely of nature,
we're continuous with whatever binds the faceless pebble, which more
    truculently persists.

Along the bladed mountains and in the deep ravines, flowers
     come forth unknown to men
and pass away unseen. When it is spring there, a thousand bloom.
     Why should this be, and for whom?

Existence must come of itself, and it goes on and on without a
     reason, just because it is.
In human consciousness, it produced an eye. It has arrived where
     it might understand. Perhaps it cannot bear this.

We have envied the crane, her clear bright wings outstretched in
     flight, that flees the dark storm cloud,
seeking a shelter, and to safe shelter, to all her shelter borne.

We have envied when we thought how in the morning light,
     gently outpoured as from a tin,
that awakens Asia's folds, some dusty marauder puts forth its claw
     and retakes the earth.

For us, all is whirled away and is vanishing, as though it were the
     sparks of a trampling flame.
A thing comes into existence if it coheres with other things, but
     this everlasting fire lives on fire, on all of itself.

The first philosophers were the best, as well as briefest.
     'Everything is metamorphosis, and nothing can remain.'
How can men have dreamed they would impose their demands
     upon the nature of this world?

There is a substance to things, which is ungraspable, unbounded;
     divided and passed on, like a secret inheritance; always
     present, in what is always passing, but never found in itself—it
     both is and is not.

Thus matter is profound; is *potentia*. And all that now exists is like the surface of the waters.

Things as they are are what is mystical. Those who search deepest are returned to life,

to ferns in a jug on the window-sill, a burned-off hillside in the dusk that is like an opal,

To a spirited horse, chrysanthemums, a pannikin that drips, creeping vines, a cut, the corners

of the mouth, a bedspread, willows, a lump, shadiness, the bowels, bright salad, and dust above distant fields.

We are given the surface again, but renewed with awe. And I remember what I have to say:

Do not believe those who have promised, in any of their ways, that something can be better than the Earth.

Although, I say this with grief for all those beings who are like shuffling, lumpy birds within a basket,

where they have spent or will spend their lives, and my heart feels suddenly stunned.

Looking out, from a verandah in the forest edge, onto tin roofs, drive-ins, supermarkets, fishing boats,

the ocean slopping by the tea-shops, the coarse cheese-rind of the beach.

The highway falls to offices and banks, to three spires (with their wrongly directed penitence).

Now the bunches of the tree-tops are rolling. A white sail has gone. Slant rain.

In the late afternoon, I read on the verandah, then look at the clear dusk.

A striped towel hangs across the rail, beside the banana palm.

A single wing on the tall sea approaches the embassy of the moon.

On South Head

The shouts of workmen at football through the twilight
from these wide, elsewhere-empty playing fields
as I walk at their wet perimeter. And the South Head light
again dumps flour on the players, and congeals,

in my head only, their stretching attitudes—
crackles their movements like static—has moved on
above a vague, cement-stiff ocean, while it extrudes
itself, quickly as a cat snatching, on the horizon.

The slingshot trajectory of that snowball flight
compacts into the furthest smoke-wall, without trace;
resumes, stiffly as a white cane, around half the night,
over youths, Laocoön for each other, on this high place,

within a wire fence along the clifftops; swinging over
water-plump lawns, rounded to their brutal deficit;
and, far off, a phantom regiment of rain. Patchy as clover,
the sea below, with mine-deep sounds. The opposite

direction, a deep gather in the landscape has banked
the city behind the players and a rickety tall goal—
stumps, fire-beaded, on a burned hillslope. This is flanked
with purple cloud and luminous plasma. And lights trail,

a long stream of sparks, among the city's gouts of light.
Matter expands or tightens, is a proto-responsiveness,
an intensity—a blowing rain with blistered sunset.
All of civilization is pre-ordained in that excess.

Impromptus

Daylight is dragged from the windows,
calling and gesturing
from further and further off. The bird's cry,
a gate closing on the plains.

*

Butterflies uplifted
above the wet-lipped grotto,
as though uttered by a St Sebastian
skewered with the sun.

*

An old treacle-sweet tune (wrapped on a spoon,
quick straps of light). Magpies must be walking about
the farmhouse lawn. And I remember how we came here under
the huge fiery litter of an autumn night.

In a vast evening, the last of daylight drifts loose
and particulate, like sugary dust
blown from a clear Arab sweet
and settling within the room's dim ultramarine.

Small Hours

I got up early, for the lavatory,
and saw the mottled yard
that was like itself in photocopy
and the moonlight fins on cloud;

then you appeared beside me and
we held a rail as travellers might,
maybe somniloquised, touched a hand,
tried to comprehend the night;

viewed it as though a tasteful grave,
until 'Nice to meet' one of us said,
who turned towards the dark wave
of our fathomless bed.

The Life of a Chinese Poet

In his youth, as he recalled, the Great Causeway of the Heavens and Earth trembled
and the stars were spilled like dust, at the overthrow of a dynasty.
It would seem that he was old from birth, who was always saying goodbye.
During eighty years he wrote five thousand poems, in a rhyming prose or as songs for the lute.
Otherwise, his life was uneventful, except for the always-remembered love that he had for a certain courtesan.
His mother refused to let him marry this girl, who was called Scented Jade,
and soon afterwards he was ordered as a minor clerk to the far province of Fukien.
There he discovered, at times, the consolation of nature—its vividness, and its unthinkable reality.
He writes of the wild mountains, that were as sharp and glittering as dog's teeth,
and that could be seen from among the hanging flowers of the white lanes.
The river there he also admired, which he says was like the great dragon of Ch'i
that turned upon itself in all the twelve directions, while subduing the five elements.

It was his dream from youth to take arms against the Golden Tartars,
but the northern frontiers had been made safe; there was no fighting, but
    only an endless boredom there.
At fifty-four, he went home to his native village, having never gained a
    preferment,
distressed by what he heard of the luxury and incontinence of the court.
He dreamed in his work of the 'vast smoke' of chariots, as they racedupon
    the plains;
he described his travels to far outposts, by night on a river that was held in
    the moon's white stare.
Though he styled himself the Hermit of the Mossy Grove, and said that
    he was wild, irascible and drunken, it seems he longed for the company
    of other poets.
He had married a local girl, when she was fifteen, and spent most of his
    time quietly lost in his books.
Pondering both the Taoist and Ch'an Buddhist teachings, he grew more
    and more enamoured of nature,
and found his companionship in mountains, rivers, and trees.
In rainy weather he would put aside his studies and trudge to the inn, to
    drink with the farming hands.
'Daily the town inn sells a thousand gallons of wine. The people are
    happy; why should I alone be sad?'
He was utterly sincere in his love of beauty. The thing he has seen appears
    on the white paper. There is a sense of overbrimming life.
A Chinese critic has said, 'His poetry has the simplicity of daily speech;
    in its simplicity there is depth, and in its poignance there is tranquillity.'
When he was seventy-one, the Mongols arose once more, and began to
    attack the Celestial Horde;
the armies of the Sung were continually defeated, and were even driven
    out of Szechuan.
Again, he applied for enlistment, but amidst the turmoil in the corridors
    at the provincial capital he was pushed aside and ignored.
Giving up all hope that before he died he would see himself in battle, he

returned to his village in disgust.
His songs were now being sung by the muleteers in far mountain
passes, by girls bringing silk to be washed in the streams.
In the capital, they were exclaimed-over at wine parties, and were
murmured beside the Imperial Lake.
He was revered, if rarely seen, in his village, but finally one morning
the word went around that he had fallen hopelessly ill.
Everything was made ready—the thin coffin, the two thick quilts, and
the payment for the monks;
the earth was thrown out of his grave onto the hillside, and the incense
was bought that would smoulder among the graveposts there.
But then, the next day, he rose on his couch, and called for wine to be
brought him from the marketplace;
he had the blind rolled up on his view to the south, and he wrote some
impeccable verses, in the tonally-regular, seven-syllable form.

Going Outside

An owl is floating
in a twilight
which has the colours
of grapefruit

painted far along
behind the pines,
those ancient spears
of serrated bone.

The fluttered breast
momentarily lit.
Maybe a dog barks
because of that.

The dog characterized
on another slope
in misty greenness
where light's draped.

And further along
the dark valley's
damp, amid the chipped
foliage of trees,

a car approaches
through severed roots
of the hills, its headlights
vanishing, coming out
.

on a wound road.
These more bright
than the owl's place
on the after-light.

'In one ear...'

In one ear
when she goes out
she'll wear,

being sixteen,
a crystal
from a chandelier,

but here
her face often hangs,
hoping it's unseen,

with a more beautiful
and far
more fierce tear.

The Sideboard

A car passes at the corner,
the damp street is silvery and still,
two of the curtains saunter
beside an open window-sill.

The living-room, silent as yet,
at my aunts'. As if it's the Ark
of the Covenant, there is set
each treasure, in the semi-dark,

on a sideboard: girls and piper
in a soap-white nude porcelain;
photographs framed with twined silver;
lacquer bowls; a blonde manikin;

a butterfly of opal; a plaster
Madonna and plastic tear.
Quietly, as if a cat burglar,
I find their lost selves in here.

The aunts, one genteel but drunken,
one with only a rat-trap thrill
livening her eyes, have forgotten
about me—gone over the hill,

both of them now, and I stay on
where red as wine old books gleam;
the light in a tortoise-shell fan;
and the cloud, a vast purple dream.

The Circus

An old and unregenerate world
is overnight unfurled
on the park—something from the fifties
and from the medieval centuries.
It has changed less than the Church,
and comes to smutch
a wealthy reserve, beside the yacht club and tennis court.
I'm walking late
when the circus appears, through our liberals' confusion.
Without flambeaux: its power generation
is on a truck. The spatulate shadows of the workmen in a foggy night
unloading at the point, by arc-light.
A ring-in myself, I have to go
on the harbour's deserted esplanade,
to watch in the dark how settlement's made.
Almost at once, I see someone throw
a hefty sodden grey tongue,
with other offal, onto the lawn—it is trailing its long
ribbons, as if a bouquet
I leave; but am back at dawn,
when the workers are already out, also unshaven.
At this hour, the faces
of the men are furtive and bitter places;
they've teeth missing, and they smoke and spit,
and are ravaged or overweight.
People line up
with buckets at a tap,
and the portable lavatories have been set up.
I'm surprised to see
a huddle of dwarfs. One comes straight across to me, truculently,
glares out of his squashed shape,
legs buckled, hair in a 'flat top',

makes an abrupt, intrusive gesture
with arm and finger,
and instructs me to piss off; then he strides
away, ignoring the duckboards.
His brow is pressed in a deep crease, beneath its curlicue,
and his wide-splayed legs
are worked like an African canoe,
where one digs
either side, heavily, to row.
Such curiosity as mine is tactless, I know.
A foetid smell
of soaked straw and dung is hung over it all.
I walk toward the morse code, jubilant water.
Here they have sat, wrapped up, backed into a corner,
one of their old men.
Life shows this kindness to some, in getting them ready for oblivion.
The harbour's the only stardust and spangles
around here, but hard to ignore the circus, as it steps from its tangles,
the tent rising like a gown. I cross to the elephants, having seen
two accidentally bump and begin a routine,
a soft shoe, in slow motion,
swaying weightlessly, as plants beneath the ocean.
Then each is once more inert,
as though dangled from a crane. They scuff with a padded foot
occasionally, and scatter chaff
in a throw-away gesture, that is like a hollow laugh.
Every inch of them is scored
as a fence's throw-away board
among sand dunes. They're clothed with tarpaulins,
and have the loose tendons
of an old man's throat. Now the skinny girls appear, whose skin
is neon white. One hangs a lurid washing, and they lean
on guy-ropes a moment in the sun
(a baby who's tripped in the mud is no-one's armful).

They're dressed for rehearsal
in fishnet tights, drawn high on their loins,
and are loose yet sinewed. Paltry as coins
it might seem, but they have the discipline of their artistry,
as well as what clichés
they share with us, of longing and hurt.
The big cats are driven out
of their cages, into the tent—the carts have been drawn up like a tail,
and the animals, goaded on, trail
through each of them, well apart, from door to open door, then
    down a wire tunnel,
crouching, as into a funnel,
to burst forth, surging upwards impressively.
The tiger's last, and it runs the cages' full length directly,
low-slung, swift as a train engine
when unencumbered, treading each piston.
It can move fast as a wasp does in attack.
One hears a whip or pistol crack
in there. The male lion, with big grassy head-dress and tapering, dried stem,
went with a heavy clearing of phlegm,
resentfully. An emblematic flower,
wilting. It is toothless, no doubt, but like Baudelaire's the rancour
of the sideways looks,
to remind of its reputation for a swordstick, of its gloveful of hooks.
Leaving, I see the old man
is dozing on. Set for a lookout, this graduand
has nothing to tell us, except to make us hope we perform
as calmly, in the face of final harm.
I look back and there is an elephant
being hosed, that's lambent;
and I wait a few minutes, to see if it wears for a hat
the day's crisp early yacht.

Impromptus

In the trail of a gypsy rain
the trees, in dripping galleries,
and sun strikes again
through a gallery of the years.

*

Love, long-burning,
although ash, remains
a perfume, invincibly
in your hair, these rooms.

*

A moth at nightfall grabs the porch light
like a man scrabbling on a slippery buoy. Shutters clash,
sand trickles out of the wall. The lemon tree's inclined
to the long curlicued whispering of the dust.

*

Lime-green all the low-beam headlight, in holiday file across
white neon of a service station. A burnt-orange dusk.
Later, the highway is a smear of grease,
and the Milky Way floats there, a feather in space.

*

With my head still lowered
at the desk, I hear
the stream again.
Is it golden now, or violet?

A Pine Forest

In autumn windows, evening's land
of ebony and fire. Out there stand
the pines, shingled on the valley,
and dark rises off them early,
exhaled across the axe-carved hills.
Above all this a vapour swirls
in the clear glass of dusk, that's lit
already with a small starlight
as highlights. That fiery moisture
is brandished, suggests a grandeur
beyond here, or a roaring wassail,
most likely, chaotic, brutal.
These pines that I gaze on arouse
disquiet in me. In early hours,
while staying here, I walk among them,
every day in a damp chasm,
a gloom. Insurgent in this country,
they're alien. 'The Ghost of a Flea',
Blake's drawing of his monstrous vision,
comes to mind. On the news station
I saw the origin of that trope—
they showed within a microscope,
like demons, fleas and other mites.
These trees recall such parasites
for me. And are, in their tight band,
too dark, too military, for a land
that naturally wears the various,
airy, open eucalyptus—
more casual, improvised things
that float their kites on loosened strings.
Under the pines, heavy needles

seem insect droppings and dead cells
coating a nest; the spiked antlers
and broken teeth, struggling creatures'
armoury; and the plated boles,
bristling, moss-infected, are scales.
Such life pronounces too gloweringly
that it's survival machinery.
Seen afar, sluggish in midday smoke,
the history that the trees evoke,
matted and drawn into a mass,
is horrible, insalubrious.
(I think of great war paintings by Dix
that one can't love, but one respects.)
The light is a fire just too far
away for harm, set where we are.

Nine poems

I sit and watch
the way rain is falling,
its eyes closed.

As if one dead
laid an arm around
your shoulders, wintry sun.

After a quarrel
she makes love in the shower
to the limbs of water.

The crows go over
all day, back and forth, anxious
to lace night with night.

Imagine dying
on this wet road; the shapeless moon
would seem so near.

A hospital room;
in the curtains, a slight breeze.
Thoughts of living.

Bring my mother in
from the morning, she will vanish
in that light.

The shadowy sides
of everything, on the way down
to the white sea.

In the vase, flowers
from deep in the heath
open their eyes.

Note

It has always seemed to me that natural things would help us
if we could hear the eloquence
of their dumb ministry.

What is it that these things of the world do?
They endure
or they flourish. They accept either, as though it were the same.

They fulfil what's given;
and they flourish, all at once, where they had seemed merely
persisting. Everything can touch them.

We are searching for the world, among something manifold
that has disposed itself
in a ramshackle system.

And our lives, we see, are just a routine sacrifice,
consumed and forgotten, off to one corner
in a courtyard of the sun.

What can last? Only what we've made
and hand on among ourselves, withered in our hands,
but never known without us.

So we take the dark roads
in beautiful clothing, greeting each other; sorry for the void
that cannot see what we've become.

Philip Hodgins
(1959-1995)

Your funeral recalled for me your poems;
I seemed to find your touch upon it all—
the trees nearby, austere, sinuous gums,
their leaves rags on barbed wire; the lustrous call
of furious magpies; clay instead of tombs;
and low weather, with dry weeds and thistle
that we came wandering over, scatteredly,
to the coffin, strung above its cavity.

The empty place the world is hung upon.
'No speeches, only verse,' in your dicta.
I read one of the pieces you had chosen,
'Sailing to Byzantium'. How bitter
the humour, the irony you implied. Then,
because there'd dried up here part of the delta
of the Murray, it seemed right that Les spoke—
spontaneously brilliant, a common bloke.

Hartley and Paul read briefly. That was all.
Backyards of wooden houses, fairly near.
Each of us dropped down that infinite hole
a flower. But first, had to stand and hear
ropes slowly creak, unwound from a steel rail—
a labour to breathe, stopping; heads bowed there.
At a mullock heap, along a gravel track,
out in Victoria, some gold put back.

You were tough-minded as a classic Roman;
vehement and pure, a believer in style;
stoic, yet glamorous like Wilfred Owen;
the exemplar of an Australian school—
going straight for the pay-dirt of emotion,
laconic, pragmatic, and sceptical.
'Live another thirty years!' If I do,
it'll seem a moment, then. I'll think of you.

Beach Shack

It's overgrown with vines, but I
push out the gritty, cracked window,
just arrived. A usual storm,
soon. Grass is ochre, even so.

A slant fence, where currawongs fall.
The east seems tar, paint-slapped thickly,
and a scalloped surf keeps passing
along the headland, radiantly.

At most times drab, now the other
white places on this slope throw back
a light that's granular, over-proof.
Broken pickets, then water's black,

on which the foam rises and soars
to land, ablaze in its spread flight.
About the yard amble warbling
those currawongs, in black and white.

To John Olsen

On your workbench were scattered some goose quills,
beside broken charcoal, inky bottles,
one not used. This a sill of twig-brushed snow,
or smoothly-threaded white sand, when the flow
of the sea's edge has left a glaze revealed.
With licked fringe, all fibres perfectly sealed,
buoyant and raked, resting at quiff and horn,
its line, as you noticed, had your guest drawn.
You trimmed the tip, to demonstrate for me
what was a draughtsman's possibility
with such implements. I saw your winged grip
put wings to your mind: every surge, each dip,
of a mountain range, far off, was caressed
by your gaze, ink proved, that space possessed.
I tried it. Perfect balance in the hand;
the hollow spine weighed by the air it fanned.
A mutation used opportunistically.
I thought of how the Sioux's famed dignity
was conferred upon them by the eagle
feathers they gathered—how not be regal
and alert, underneath those crowns they wore.
I glimpsed this, while you urged me on to draw,
and dipping with that heroic billow,
traced the bleached draperies beyond Lithgow.
'Look at that,' you cried, and presented me
the instrument of such discovery.
I wanted then to continue to ply
that great quill, felt imperious as Bligh,
possessed by a sagacity like Cook's,
but there was more to learn—turned to your works,
and found among them their diversity.

I admired a more languid quality
in your brushwork; so Aboriginal
its ease, its slowness; this the very style
of our impassive land: like campfire smoke,
eucalypt boughs, shorelines, creeks. You evoke
a Chinese spirit, too—the passive strengths
of earth and water is in those great lengths
your lines sustain, as time, then timelessness.
How Taoist, the reins you give to looseness,
and tauten, just where you need. You've the skills
that suit this place. Your marks become tendrils
of waterlilies, inky waterholes,
the fur of caterpillars, the great boles,
slowly surging, of gum trees, scribbled knots
of foliage, speckled pond-life, mallee roots.
These trails, watery or tarred, are aerial
as native art: concepts, yet sensual.
Your project's to 'write the landscape' for us,
newcomers and reserved, and a chorus
in your talk is, 'Drawing is empathy.'
This was at lunch, with wine deployed freely
for all but strong Michael, who was driver.
Outdoors, under crumbling wisteria,
crumbling our bread; the peacock's display
stalking us. Formerly a seminary,
your place's casements open on the foam
of acres of roses, on pine groves, a dome
of hill above, doodled with scrub, a line
of jet's vapour angled behind. The wine
encouraged my playful provocation,
that drawing's design. 'It's superstition,'
you said, 'sympathetic magic—the edge
that primitive Picasso had.' You allege

it's always accidents. Your mind's pliant
as your line: our elder, you're complainant
against all rigidities, including
the modernistic—cubist fracturing
you much deride. 'Every emphasis
in art means loss. Who can talk of progress?'
On our way home, I drooped in the back seat,
all windows down, struck by long shafts of heat.
Through the Blue Mountains, in raiding traffic;
less art nouveau forest each year, more brick.
Your feather lay lightly as a Nile boat
beside me—next thing, I saw it afloat
upon a flood tide; snatched out by the draught
a stampeding truck had made. 'Plucked,' I laughed
ruefully, 'a last time.' The truck was gone,
its wheels revolving like sawmill blades, on
down the highway, in free fall, with my quill
riding its slipstream, a windsurfer's sail;
on gilded air, blue smoke-burst eucalypts,
the feather's cursiveness; its catch at slips;
a rapier exploring; arabesques
above the cars ahead (I loved those risks);
then flung to the bush, defiant ensign.
I said, 'I wish John could have seen that line.'

Wintry Dusk, Bellingen

There's a cellophane dimness to the world.
Three white cockatoos are raucous over
the moon's ulcerous face, that's now revealed.
Across the paddocks is passed a shiver;
and down through deep grass the dark fence-posts ride.
Pointing everywhere, the dead trees gesture,
as if they were in panic when they died.

Visiting in Fife

Through the nylon curtains
one other bungalow,
a road, a wood, some pegs afloat,
the grass and tea-towel blow.

A long road from bare hills;
a close wood, dark as mint.
His days are lard that's smeared
on torn bits of newsprint.

These damp trees, too, like days
packed together that hunch
and sway as a boxer
does, waiting with a punch.

After Heraclitus

Late to lie awake
in a borrowed house in the country
in a forest of rain,
hearing its fine
traffic or the deeply held tone
of cello strings
softly drawn.
One knows oneself at this hour:
the range is guilt
or obsession with loss or fearfulness or fear
for another. One lies
drenched in thought.
The human is excess

of consciousness. For me
it has been the hands and feet
caught below the gunwale
from the dark
and I trying to pull those figures up
out of the waters—
they become inert;
they are unable to come in.
And there are others; although with them
it is they and not I
want possession;
and they are limber. I have been
unlatching them,
not too unkindly, I would like to think,
but over and again. 'You will make it
on your own,' I say;
'it's overloaded here,
we'll sink.' Having to push away
faces I've known
or have loved. Economies
are imposed upon the heart.
I take up a book
and wish the day would break.
Even the tight
bulrushes, under the boughs
along the creek,
will be soaked full by now,
sopping in the warp
of lightning. A shimmer
from the garden—
the rubber gloves drawn on.
Women are nature's victims,
and we're theirs, and they are ours.

What rockets, what shout,
what furies
of hurt, what adhesive fire.
And wrapping itself
about itself, the ancient rain
comes reeling through the paddocks.
How exaggerated
one's regrets
are in the crisis, the crossing point,
of night. At daybreak
I lie on the floor
of an entangled pond, looking up
through the murk
to where the web-foot
leaves are treading
the surface, in dimness. I understand
'it is death for the soul
to grow sodden.'
I hear what could seem
a paper umbrella, being tapped upon
with a Japanese
sparsity and calm. The sun
is able to kindle
in such a soaking world again.
'The sleepers dream
in a world which is each their own,
but the daylight world
is ours in common.'
One steps into the river
as a river. Within an hour
I walk in the garden, hung around
by mulberry, persimmon,
palms with low fronds,

and oleander. In their shade
stand, more scintillant
than Manhattan's night, from an airline
flight, all these grass-tall spires
of rain. The wattle
that's clothed in spindled
leaves is thickly starred
with a shaggy bright water
as though it were the Milky Way.
I try to picture
how the light takes everywhere it rides,
across the valleys, across the hills—
those uncounted cells
of water, which are seeds.
There's a fruit lit
in the lap of each leaf, at the tip
of every black stick.
The close fields
are as ripe as oil paint; the longueurs
of the pastures
still wrapped in smoke.
In a wind, higher up
on the ridge, the tree-line is deciduous
as a clarinet.
Steam rises in the forest gate.
How this light exceeds Corot's
unshakeable dew. We know
there's no pause
to the brute secateurs,
and yet we must think Hail.
'Hail, holy light,'
although it's not the offspring
of Heaven's son—it is the lightning

from the start of time,
and our blessedness,
even as it keeps the nature of flame.

In Departing Light

My mother all of ninety has to be tied up
on her wheelchair, but still she leans far out of it sideways;
she juts there brokenly,
able to cut
with the sight of her someone who is close. She is hung
like her hanging mouth
in the dignity
of her bleariness, and says that she is
perfectly all right. It's impossible to get her to complain
or to register anything
for longer than a moment. She has made Stephen Hawking look
healthy.
It's as though
she is being sucked out of existence sideways through a porthole
and we've got hold of her feet.
She's very calm.
If you live long enough it isn't death you fear
but what life can still do. And she appears to know this somewhere,
even if there's no hope she could speak of it.
Yet she is so remote you think of an immortal—a Tithonus withering
forever on the edge
of life,
although with never a moment's grievance. Taken out to air,
my mother seems in a motorcycle race, she
the sidecar passenger
who keeps the machine on the road, trying to lie far over

beyond the wheel.
Seriously, concentrated, she gazes ahead
toward the line,
as we go creeping around and around, through the thick syrups
of a garden, behind the nursing home.
Her mouth is full of chaos.
My mother revolves her loose dentures like marbles ground upon each other,
or idly clatters them,
broken and chipped. Since they won't stay on her gums
she spits them free
with a sudden blurting cough, which seems to have stamped out of her
an ultimate breath.
Her teeth fly into her lap or onto the grass,
breaking the hawsers of spittle.
What we see in such age is for us the premature dissolution of a body
that slips off the bones
and back to protoplasm
before it can be decently hidden away.
And it's as though the synapses were almost all of them broken
between her brain cells
and now they waver about feebly on the draught of my voice
and connect
at random and wrongly
and she has become a surrealist poet.
'How is the sun
on your back?' I ask. 'The sun
is mechanical,' she tells me, matter of fact. Wait
a moment, I think, is she
becoming profound? From nowhere she says, 'The lake gets dusty.' There is
  no lake
here, or in her past. 'You'll have to dust the lake.'
It could be
that she is, but then she says, 'The little boy in the star is food,'

or perhaps 'The little boy is the star in food,'
and you think, More likely
this appeals to my kind of superstition—the sleepless, inspiring homunculus.
It is all a tangle and interpretation,
a hearing amiss,
all just the slipperiness
of her descent.
We sit and listen to the bird-song, which is like wandering lines
of wet paint—
it is like an abstract expressionist at work, his flourishes and
then
the touches
barely there,
and is going on all over the stretched sky.
If I read aloud skimmingly from the newspaper, she immediately falls
asleep.
I stroke her face and she wakes
and looking at me intently she says something like, 'That was
a nice stick.' In our sitting about
she has also said, relevant of nothing, 'The desert is a tongue.'
A red tongue?'
'That's right, it's a
it's a sort of
you know—it's a—it's a long
motor car.'
When I told her I might be in Cambridge for a while, she told me,
'Cambridge is a very old seat of learning. Be sure—'
but it became too much—
'be sure
of the short Christmas flowers.' I get dizzy,
nauseous,
when I try to think about what is happening inside her head. I keep her
out there for hours, propping her

straight, as
she dozes, and drifts into waking; away from the stench and
the screams of the ward. The worst
of all this, to me, is that despite such talk, now is the most peace
I've known her to have. She reminisces,
momentarily, thinking I am one of her long-dead
brothers. 'Didn't we have some fun
on those horses, when we were kids?' she'll say, giving
her thigh a little slap. Alzheimer's
is nirvana, in her case. She never mentions
anything of what troubled her adult years—God, the evil passages
of the Bible, her own mother's
long, hard dying, my father. Nothing
at all of my father,
and nothing
of her obsession with religion, that he drove her to. She says the magpie's
    song,
that goes on and on, like an Irishman
wheedling to himself,
which I have turned her chair towards,
reminds her of
a cup. A broken cup. I think that the chaos in her mind
is bearable to her because it is revolving
so slowly—slowly
as dust motes in an empty room.
The soul? The soul has long been defeated, and is all but gone. She's only
    productive now
of bristles on the chin, of an odour
like old newspapers on a damp concrete floor, of garbled mutterings, of
some crackling memories, and of a warmth
(it was always there,
the marsupial devotion), of a warmth that is just in the eyes, these days,
    particularly

when I hold her and rock her for a while, as I lift her
back to bed—a folded
package, such as,
I have seen from photographs, was made of the Ice Man. She says,
'I like it
when you—when
when
you…'
I say to her, 'My brown-eyed girl.' Although she doesn't remember
the record, or me come home
that time, I sing it
to her: 'Sha lala
la la lala … And
it's you, it's you'-she smiles up, into my face—'it's you, my brown-eyed girl.'
My mother will get lost on the roads after death.
Too lonely a figure
to bear thinking of. As she did once,
one time at least, in the new department store
in our town; discovered
hesitant among the aisles; turning around and around, becoming
a still place.
Looking too kind
to reject outright
even a wrong direction. And she caught my eye, watching her,
and knew I'd laugh
and grinned. Or else, since many another spirit will be arriving over there,
    whatever
those are—and all of them clamorous
as seabirds, along the walls of death—she will be pushed aside
easily, again. There are hierarchies in Heaven, we remember; and we know
of its bungled schemes.
Even if 'the last shall be first,' as we have been told, she
could not be first. It would not be her.

But why become so fearful?
This is all
of your mother, in your arms. She who now, a moment after your game,
    has gone;
who is confused
and would like to ask
why she is hanging here. No—she will be safe. She will be safe
in the dry mouth
of this red earth, in the place
she has always been. She
who hasn't survived living, how can we dream that she will survive her
death?

Thomas Hardy

    Tender-hearted
    and affronted
by the Arbiter of this world—
    you yourself had
    been made stunted

    yet romantic;
    you'd erotic
longings, and these were always foiled.
    Your aesthetic
    was the Gothic

    and gratitude
    for a girl's nude
shoulder, or female shape, though furled—
    things too valued,
    too long pursued.

Looks in debit
and short on wit;
no easy talk. Intense glance hurled
had for target
how bosoms sit.

Yet, the poet
transcended that:
with Donne and Wordsworth you're enrolled,
a lyric great
of English Lit.

Always lustful,
unsuccessful,
your complaint, Injustice, unrolled,
become general,
in volumes-full

on dead Heaven.
And forgiven,
by you, were those whom you'd repelled.
For you, shriven
all the women,

except only
one not comely
any more—ego brittle-shelled,
grown bitterly
fat and lonely.

And she, your wife,
    was also rife
for God's team. But you would have healed,
    such your warm life,
    all other strife.

In the Mallee

This is the kind of bush that one might have hoped
not to see; certainly,
while prepared to do it once, it's not the bush you would choose again
to come trampling amongst.
The heat here is a heavy weight.
If you stop,
straight away the big ants pour upwards over your boots,
jointed, globular and
stilted like
the mechanical explorers of another world. The sky is grey with heat
and looks as though dust
evaporates,
but the earth is the rust on iron plates.

Sparse trees
spread their branches immediately off the ground (their economy)
and have sparse
dim tags
for leaves. They seem just upright shadows. And the pale blue-grey
salt bushes, clumped
and low, appear
to be gas flames, in
the dry wind,
on a flatness that is equal everywhere.

This is the sort of harshness
that helped give Henry Lawson, with secret heart, the horrors. It
   is this place
reconciled Shaw Neilson
to his near-blindness; who said while labouring here on the road
that he wasn't much interested
in views,
anyway. It gave him an 'inner life'. I am walking to where, like some
   geological fracture,
big trees arise, tarnished silver,
with their scattered scratching of leaves.
They're in a brittle scrubland that encloses
the khaki waters
of the Murray;

on reaching which, I throw a twig in
to see if it moves. It does,
eventually, or it seems to, if that was not a breeze. These eucalyptus
lean from both banks
(the water a hundred metres wide) with a calcified
stiffness. They are hung all about in shreds;
their bark worse
in appearance than even their blight is—those vast
termite nests, high on the boles
of many. I always think of
Ghirlandio's portrait of the old man
with a diseased nose, on seeing such growths. Endlessly
touching, these old men. 'Eternal passion,
eternal pain,' as Matthew Arnold
said, of the nightingale (although the passion here
has dried into endurance). An appropriate
prompting, nevertheless, since this too seems the pain
of the bereft.

I decide to head back
for the road, which is over where the birds slowly rise and settle
in a flock, a black
basketball's tumbling, slow-
motion bounce. These are the eagles and their consorts, now,
the crows, which are forced to move
together, and to quarrel,
along the gravel
verge, since the rabbits again
have been the subject of our vendetta and are gone.

As I leave the river bank and start off through the dust and trash
of this camp site,
as it might seem, among
the sticks, ashen leaves, fallen
boughs, old
logs, blady grass, bracken, there is a crackling and
a young fox
is here, although moving away fast—has already gone past me, fast
and cool,
on small corgi legs, low
in the sand. Not so much
trotting, as drawn on little wheels,
sedate.
It is flowing away obliquely, with an averted
shy face; the nostrils
held up slightly, and seeming to ask
a complicity
in non-recognition; or its head could be held there in a mild
disdain. Mild
like steel, I think, if it is making a living
out here. It's
spruce and neat, perfectly

elongated—there is a flourishing, easy
health about
this predator. Its hair
is flowing back lightly all around it, the orange
of a Dutchman's beard. Or, there's
an elegance to this creature, that looks as though the mannequin and her fur
have been resolved into one.

A hedgerow moisture, to its brightness.
The fox's being able to live at its ease, at least until recently, in exile here
from soggy England, makes it seem
an anomaly
in nature, something
gratuitous—the excess
from which things have evolved. It is as though
Neilson's delicacy, or Lawson's tenderness,
had flourished in their time.

Damp Evening

Faintly lit by the leaf-muffled streetlights, or by lights in the house-fronts,
the rain that has fallen here wildly now picks itself up with the weariness
of smoke.

Steeply downhill, when I look back, a lighted ferry moves below the
ruin-shaped, dark tree-line on the far side of the bay, heading out into a
vast mulberry-coloured harbour.

This stockily-built ferry is all that moves, sliding transversely to the
plunging line of the street. It is as tightly packed with light as a truck
with bales of hay. Around it is scattered, entangled and kinked, the loose
straws of its load.

Above the ferry and the low headland is a view of the city, of suburbs
and towers, receding on black promontories, as though displayed upon

variously extended screens. What is depicted there is a jungle façade, filled with the eyes of creatures that have come down to a riverbank.

And then, farther still, there lies open the last of a brocade sunset, in watery splendour. The edge of its light is earthed by three tall palm trees, to the small park at the bottom of the street. Or those trees are fan-shaped, long-handled watercolour brushes that have been laid neatly aside and have bled brilliantly onto a dark ground. Their paint makes appear strange uplands, among which are purple forests, vermilion and lime-green lakes, and a gold-leafed pavilion. Within that sky there is a further sky, of apricot.

The eye lowers from such vistas and finds the ferry, out on the open water. It's become a homely trader's wagon, trudging toward the edge of the steppe.

And the last of the wet sunset seems now some marvellous voice, high and steady, that is fading away within the throat of darkness.

Thirteen poems

Flesh-pale boards
and scaffolding. A distant train.
The rock dreams a tree of stars.

Going home, through steep
woods, the water limps
from stone to stone.

Moon, a spinnaker
on the bay of night, and stars
are a distant shore.

On the pond, raindrops
open, big as lily-pads.
The barn's shadow. Dusk.

Thick sunset waters,
golden as whisky. In this light
the tree-roots will walk.

The kettle, as it
begins to boil (him!), lowers
and lowers its voice.

In the dim room
a piano-lid propped. Urgent
sail, far from home.

Darkness, road lights.
Walking down, around the valley—
joining-up what shape?

Late afternoon sun
in the back of the shed,
cornered and still.

A dim road, leaf-stained,
near the lake. In the headlights,
the screen door ajar.

The sky, thick with stars,
is the floor of a saucepan
that's about to boil.

Open the door on
the gunshot of the morning—
work all day wounded.

The eagles are dust
in heaven. The kitchen's lit.
Cobwebs, sweat drops.

The Drift of Things

Things, Berkeley says, are the language of God,
the world we are given is really His thought,
which Hume remarked brings us no conviction,
yet to me it is almost justified,
for things are worthy of such existence,
of ultimate standing. They're the location
of all we know. Nothing duplicitous
in that vulnerability; we can sense
they are present entire. It feels these things
that step through the days with us have the fullness,
in each occasion, of reality.

A wharf among reeds and clouds on water;
the bus that rides the dust like a surfboard;
a lizard, tail hung from the mailbox drum,
inert, all a long-shadowed afternoon;
the planks on mud, from where chickens' pollard
is thrown; the scatterings of cherry bloom,
as white as the Sabine women; a star
at dusk, that's dripping wet; or the avenue
of trees, to exalted snow…each is itself
and no other thing. It's plurality

we experience; it is differences,
not the smear of Oneness, the haecceity
that we knew as children. Glad animals,
for us phenomena were then enough;
we took variety and relations
as literally, we'd find out later,
as William James had enjoined us to do.
We were so awed, so entranced, in childhood
by objects' insistence, to us they've seemed
sufficient. Ordinary particulars
as basic existence was something that we'd
have agreed with Aristotle about.

And these things flow into one another
as quietly as smoke, unhesitant,
unhampered. Glittering smoke of the world.
The differences among them don't exclude
their coherence; their unity doesn't
detract from difference. Still, there can't be
some fundamental underneath all this
that has remained itself, and that is 'pure.'
All things change: where could there be a refuge?
What can be sequestered from existence?
Something inert would be the same as nothing.
Since the world's substance is in flux, it means
there is no Substance; things always vary
on the one level of reality.
What the world is made of are the things that
it existed as before. Responding
is its principle. And all existence,
like an acrobat, will tumble over
again and again, each time it should fall.

Or it's a sweltering ocean; the waves
of things flow through each other endlessly.

Those one hundred and sixty million years
of the dinosaurs, which spent all their days
ravening on each other, must imply
the God of this is monstrous, too, or bored,
or was suffering then from crazy nightmares—
is something absurd. And life's been blown to
a lucky shore in time; and if it's not
entirely so, there are times within Time
and places that seem to us sanctified.

As religion wanted us to believe,
some thinkers taught us, that we cannot know.
Yet the minute fine co-ordination
of the senses to nature, cell by cell,
has been the sole project of our animal
evolution, to now. Between one thing
and another, where is there obstruction?
What is the use in 'representations'?
Our hands and feet must have freedom to act;
if someone should fumble a precious bowl
we've caught it, split second, we don't know how.
The body has its bias, to survive;
nothing intrudes between the world and that,
but wordless perception takes care of all.
Such an account allows mistakes occur;
the mistakes we make prove there is a world.

So consciousness, quicker than thought, is thin:
as Sartre said, it is 'as thin as nothing',
or as the nerves registering on the brain.

The 'mind' reveals the body to itself:
it only can present; body responds.
The body can do more than we have dreamed.
A human is a thing that's self-reflexive
(this luminescence casts us into darkness).
Our consciousness is like a fine spotlight
that's focused on just one place at a time:
we notice when we hear that we don't see,
that there's ear-consciousness, eye-consciousness,
and so on, interchanging very fast.
Hearing rain, we don't feel the wooden chair,
and in thinking we close out stimuli.
What is the 'knower' but a passing thought
that's counted there amongst experience?
The consciousness one takes to be oneself
is, in fact, completely impersonal:
'Everything's outside it…even our thoughts.'

But the world we're given is stolen from us
we live with fear of loss, like Orpheus.
What our senses tell us we must deny:
that flux can't be accepted, even by science,
which keeps a 'spiritual' prejudice.
The essences it seeks are just in thought;
electrons and the like aren't absolute,
do not exist apart, they're not 'more real'
than houses are and trees, mountains and clouds;
all of this co-exists, as one event.
It's complexity that's fundamental.

An image from the Flower Garland Sutra—
existence is a web of diamonds,
and within each faceted stone there's hung

the rest of the net, as its reflections.
A thing is caused by all else in the world;
it hasn't a fixed nature, self-defined;
there is just relativity—'emptiness'.
It's because each thing is correlative
that each opens for us a hundred gates
upon the ocean of the world's meaning.
The world is the mutual dependence
of every separate fact and point of view.

As change is real, so qualities are, also.
No qualities exist apart from mass,
and there's no mass that's without 'properties'.
Things are not thin, like thought. They've density.
A thing is what distinguishes itself.
It is at once arbitrary and absolute.
The quantity these have is never lost:
their mass, as such, is the ungraspable,
the ungrounded; one could say it is God,
but a God that doesn't want to be God.
All of its content is found 'outside' it.
Things borrow their fullness from each other,
so what they each are made of is Existence.
It's here the commonplace becomes sublime.
We see the streetlights in the summer dusk,
as if they're why we came to live on Earth
(with earthquakes, hurricanes, and viruses).

When we are queued for the banks of Lethe
we'll recall, attentive as candle flame,
not only faces, but things we have known,
and with an intensity that is surprised—
the stance of grass at the foot of palings

one storm-lit afternoon; the night, an ocean
among its ice-floes; whatever flung us
into the furthest transcendence we found.
We will see the world as a great forest,
an undergrowth of things that is solemn
and remote, and arduous, impassive,
as the land that rises before us there.
Things were prophetic of such mystery:
they were always the flowerings of Hades.

But this is metaphor. No-one endures.
What strikes us most of things is their strangeness,
and how speak of that, but through metaphor?
In seeing things now, it's as if they're lost
already. They've seemed to me a pathos,
whether met calmly or in exultance.
They pass us along the edge of darkness,
are glimpsed from highways, changing as we're changed.

The trees wear peculiar significance
in their stance on a hilltop or a plain:
these things that are more than just what is found.
The nature of matter is an Abyss.

Behind a shed, low ridges, and great clouds;
a gravel lane; pale sun on dusty grass;
the broken palings and the wire netting;
a gate, into a dimly-veined forest;
the canal with swallow. Marvellous phantoms.
All thought fails before their attendance here.

A Bowl of Pears

Swarthy as oilcloth and as paunched
as Sancho Panza
wearing a beret's little stalk
the pear

itself suggests the application of some rigour
the finest blade
from the knife drawer
here

to freshen it is one slice and then another
the north fall south fall
facets of glacier
the snow-clean juice with a slight crunch that is sweet

I find lintels and plinths of white marble
clean angled
where there slides
the perfume globule

a freshness
like the breeze that is felt upon
the opening
of day's fan

Enku
sculptor of pine stumps
revealed the ten thousand Buddhas with his attacks
the calligraphic axe

Rationalised shape shaped with vertical strokes
I have made of your jowled

buttocks
a squareness neatly pelvic

A Sunday of rain
and like a drain
a pipe that was agog and is now chock-a-block the limber
thunder
rebounds and bounds

it comes pouring down
a funnel the wrong way around
broadcasts
its buffoon militance over the houses all afternoon

Undone
the laces of rain
dangle on the windows
now slicing iron

a butcher is sharpening
the light
of his favourite knife
its shimmers carving stripes into the garden

And I have carved the pear-shaped head
with eyes
close set
as pips that Picasso saw his poor

friend who had gone
to war
a cubist
snowman the fragrant and fatal Apollinaire

The Fishermen

There comes trudging back across the home paddocks of the bay,
pushing its way
waist-deep in the trembling seed-heads of the light,
a trawler, with nets aloft
and a motor that thumps like an irrigation pump
on the monolithic cloud. That cloud is straining out the sunrise
of a Bible tract,
and shows a few lumps of islands and one boat
in the blazing sand-box of the sea,
while close-up the edges of such a volatile grit
are being swept ashore.
It is all noticed by someone in pyjama stripes
and venetian slats of light,
at one of the wide bungalows
above the wind-moulded scrub, by two early walkers going down a track
onto the dunes,
from where they will watch the baggy sea that is practising its
ju-jitsu on the kelp.

Only the harsh approval of the gulls
that the fishermen are back, the small boat
swimming heavily with nose up,
after a night far out on the phosphorescent plain, in a seething culture
of hatching snake eggs, or from deep
in an icy slush
of moonlight, the sea corrosive-smelling
and raw like rust. Back from the cobra-flaring,
gliding and striking sea, goaded it would seem by their presence there,
who tear
up by the roots the nets and lobster traps;
from a sea sweaty with stars, or one black and flowing like crepe;

a sea that erupts
and falls on them so hugely that only the radio mast could have shown
in the foam, if they'd had one. The fishermen have been taught
by each other that if swept away
in such a sea, without a jacket, which they don't wear in their work
to swim down and make an end of it,
since they will never get back.
They live inside a dream
out there; everything they know about is in shadow,
who sometimes see a liner,
further off, go drifting past them like a town
on the moon,
and who see the ocean vomit a black whale
as if that were its tongue.

But you have come back, the pair of you, to a morning world
of newspapers and washed cement,
to swollen, damp
milk cartons, and car fumes,
to a train that comes hobbling through the edge of town,
past wooden tenements, with sand hung
in their eyebrows,
and a sky like bacon.

One of you has a wife, and she is brusque, earth-bound, and
    unforgiving still.
She loves you, you can tell, by her sullen glances.
Her humid-smelling nightgown
and the smoky curlicues of hair about her ears, in the steaming light—.
'Don't empty those boots there!
What the hell's
the matter with that kid? Give him
to me. Why must you always have this bloody soup for your breakfast?

Look,
I'm burning it again. Do something:
watch it. No,
that toast is for the children!'

Who can know how strange the land is for you,
the place where you come to sleep?
You have watched the single mass of the mountains worked loose
that goes down aslant into the Underworld,
and alone then in the bow have seen the bear paws
of the ocean idly claw at you.

You see now, half-asleep, the children eating—the grain comes undone
in their mouths,
and you don't speak, you watch your hands, you once slapped one
like a wave.
And then you wake,
and all is silent. You stagger, scratching
at your underwear. The little cells of the screen door
in the afternoon sun sealed with dust. Those big lemons, breast-tipped,
are new on that young tree, out alone in the concrete yard. On the table
the shopping lies agape
like a mouth of grief—the tins of tomatoes, red molars; the foam of the
    bread.
You give up, quite soon, tinkering with the bath-heater
and write on the back of a note
a note, with a pen that half works. You walk through the glare
like someone taking a sick day, to the pub,
and again join the idlers there
in swallowing fumes and shadows.
The school kids come out shrieking in the sun—
such animals, you see, as you have released from your body,
in the hope of a little comfort, a home. What a delusion

that was. Children were to keep a woman busy
until you returned. In the pub, you stagger before you can walk again
on the water.
It is time to go out
with this bastard, your old mate.
You look up at him, where he comes to get you—his face
might have been some woman's nightmare;
a breath of sour acids,
and never a tender intonation to his voice.
You take your mate's hand, that is hard as a damp stone,
reached to you on the floor,
in the gutter,
in the sea. Through his broken teeth he tells you
to hold on, you will be all right. He pulls you into the boat
or he'll come out himself.
It can never be said, but you think, Where
have you found a love like this? In the morning, you and he separate
    once more,
with a few curt words
at the jetty.
You turn and walk inland, along the gravel, and pause sometimes, amid
the scaffolding of the day.

Shack and Pine Tree

Here I could write of an afternoon in a sailboat on the lake. It
would be a high place in the history of sleep. And here you'd speak
again of an evening in your own tongue, which is a dialect of the
rain.

Home Run

The first time that you see the ocean from the North Coast line
is a place I have passed
very often;
it is 'the prized, the desired sight,'
unearned, uncaught, that 'parts me leaf from leaf';
nowhere seems to me more beautiful,
except maybe
the country between Gloucester and Dungog:
these are the kingdom of God
on Earth, especially
in the late or early sun. You know that you'll arrive soon
at this place on the coast, the first ingress…although, I am wrong.
I'm remiss;
there is a glimpse of the sea
and of an estuary, before that; no matter…you know you will
    soon come to the place I mean
when you've left Nambucca
and on either side there is a forest of paperbarks
in a swamp or reed-bed,
birch-like
saplings, long and thin, that push up
tightly together, and are glimmering, in the softness of the preferred hour.
Although, these can seem, rather,
to descend, with their slight wave rings; to be runnels
of watery gouache,
the cream
of dampened woodash,
on charcoal-dim
slanted paper—long dribblings
from out of the amorphous, smoky, olive mass
of their foliage.

And lying among these trees, you will see, is a creek
with many tendrils, like a root,
appearing everywhere, through acres of long grass, a seemingly
    broken water,
coloured like the water
we washed our brushes in at school.
Here you often slow almost to a stop
and roll above the swamp;
a slow tread
on the levee, the rail-bed,
while to the right the creek suddenly becomes a small lake, from
beneath your feet.
In fact, it's an estuary,
hidden around a corner from the ocean. Across that light-sealed water
is a red clay bank
steep as a hillslope, with cursory, white, long-stemmed ideograms, very
    finely done,
scattered over it, the boles and limbs
of twisted gums, and the clumps
of their foliage a pale blue mildew. So you pass
through the ghostly melaleucas
with their strangely wadded, loose-leafed bark,
which looks sodden and plumped,
but is a worm-eaten, dry, clay-white parchment. (Though if you take off
an easy handful of it,
there is a mushroom-pink or a peach-toned
delicate tinge
to its inner side: it is beautifully silk-lined.) You pass over a trestle
slowly, and begin to rush
again, through a close bush, among its scratched graffiti and chipped
paint, before that's rent
like curtains billowing open; and there, dazzling as the shock
of lifted plumes—light-speckled, and with a high-pitched note,

it might seem,
it's so bright—
is the ocean.
This, after all night on the frowsty train, feeling half-sozzled,
sealed-in, air-conditioned,
and tasting of aluminium. One sees it
'silent upon a peak in Darien.'
But the train leaps on
curving through the bush, inland now, like a dog off the chain,
into the clean,
lean dairying country; among the cleared paddocks that stage
the eloquence
of their single great trees,
to a massed audience of new-growth forest, shadow-faced.
This bright, mown country is being transformed by light that steams
above the forest,
as a piece of toast is with its butter.
The long ramps
of the burnished grass lead away, towards a far-off plateau, a jacket on a
chair-back.
And there appears an empty road, which we shoulder up against
and jostle aside,
our only rival, and it hares off, free,
not to be bothered,
weaving fast, unfazed, unslackening. It is the dusty
appealing colour of rolled-out dough.
And the grass, close by,
is the colour of powdered malt, or in some places the sable
of a Burmese cat.
The braggart light is on stilts now.
You pass into a forest again, of glass-deep
shadows, among glass
reflections—the gum tree saplings, in a myriad white long stripes.

These are a downpour
that is splashing up ferns. The forest has the many curved forms
of cluttering umbrellas
afloat. And now, more bright pastures, although barely any cattle in sight:
they can hide, the paddocks are so billowing and vast,
in the warmer hollows. And here again is the lapsing and picked-up thread
of fine
lit telephone line.
It is like the swallows that come along with us; their progress,
as that of a porpoise.
But still, the first time that you see the ocean
from the North Coast train
is the great tune
in this production.
Of all the colour, this is the colour to have seen. The sea
is blue as ink,
or as a dye, newly pulped,
from out of which a great billow of fabric has been lifted,
the slightly lighter sky.
The light cells seem to exchange their energy, where they are lying on the
    ocean in long
transverse peninsulas,
so rapidly
that each photon is no sooner spent than it's re-lit
at the end of its quantum flicker. The beach is white
as a tablet of bath soap. There is a knoll
or sand dune
in the middle of the scene
from the top of which the long grass streams, something inexpressibly felt.
The waves stoop
with the shoulders of sea eagles and the gull-white feathers burst.
And you notice how the wind-paths, beyond the breakers, run out
    across the water,

sinuous and spreading, like the arms
of the open eucalypts.

from
Nameless Earth (2006, 2009)

Flying Foxes

In the night, the gorging begins again, in the spring
night, in the branches
of the Moreton Bay figs,
that are fully-rigged
as windjammers, and make a flotilla along the street.
And from the yard-arms
are strung clusters
of hanged sailors,
canvas-wrapped and tarred—these are the bats, come
for the split fruit, and dangled,
overturned where they land.
It is the tobacco fibrils
in the fruit they seek,
and those berries, when gouged,
are spilled, through the squall
of the crowd, like
a patter of faeces
on the bitumen. This amidst
the cloudy shine
of the saline
streetlamps. In the ripe nights
the bats fumble and waste
what they wrest—
there's a damp paste
upon the road,
which dries to matted
sawdust, soon after the day's
steam has reared; it is scraped
up by the shovel-load.
The bats are uncorked
like musty vapour, at dusk,

or there is loosed a fractured
skein of smoke, across
the embossed lights
of the city. The moon is lost,
to an underhanded
flicked long brush-load of paint.
You think of the uncouth ride
of the Khan and his horde,
their dragon-backed shape
grinding the moon
beneath its feet.
And of an American
anthem, the helicopters
that arrive with their *whomp whomp*
whomp. I'm woken
by the bats still carrying on
in the early hours,
by the outraged screech
and thrashing about
where they clamber heavily
as beetles do on each other's backs.
They extend
a prosthetic limb,
snarl, and knuckle-walk
like simians, step
each other under
or chest-beat, although
hampered with a cape. In sleep
I trample the bedsheet
off, and call out
'Take that!' (I am told),
punching the pillow in the heat.
I see the fanged shriek

and the drip
of their syringes,
those faces with the scowl
of a walnut kernel.
It's some other type of bat
I think of: these, in books,
where I look them up,
have a face you can imagine
if you recall how you'd whittle
finely at a pencil
and moisten the lead
with the tongue-tip
a little face that belies its greed,
like that of an infant.
All partly autonomous things
trample others down,
even what is their own,
and the whole earth is ground
or smoulders
with pain. No comfort for us that
of a night I have seen
how the living pass
about the earth,
that is deep in the ashes
of the dead, and quickly, too,
vanish into dark,
like will-o'-the-wisps
thrown out of the sun.
At three o'clock I gather
our existence
has been a mistake. I would like
to turn my back on
its endless strife;

but when I look out
at the night, I am offered
otherwise only
the chalk-white
and lacklustre moon.

To a Friend

The sun is burning the edge of the western hills,
they're charred like newspaper that is used for a torch;
a moon has strewn its litter through the wet valley,
beside the road, and where that branches in the yard.
Water birds leave this place at the ends of the earth,
and smoke from the farms is stretching out on the lake.
All day I have wandered barefoot from room to room,
and maybe I've written at least one new poem,
after a long wait. I'm uncertain, however,
on whom I can try it. Not with fax or e-mail,
if I had them, P.H., could I send it to you.
I used to call you that for your exact opinions—
someone who's dying young will at best become sharp.
You'd have told me if I wasted my time today,
and you might have been moved to write something, also.
In writing, it wasn't renown I was after;
it seemed more an offering to one's ancestor.
You thought, too, that art's apogee was long ago.

At the Cove

Early morning and I hang footloose in the ocean, out beyond the breakers. My legs could be seaweed tendrils, inside water that's a green smoke.

The suburb, set steeply above the beach, is obscured, as if it were an audience across the footlights. Already, hot sun reaches along the sea, and gathers between those dark brick bungalows the broken pieces of last night's rain, as bright vapour.

On the tented sea is a brilliant frost. Among its thin, strewn brocades, the water's ultramarine, much darker than the sky, which is a cobalt blue and unadulterated by any cloud. In salty eyes, the light becomes dazzling geometries, as when a cinematic lens shoots into the sun.

The wobbly sea makes me feel I am treading in the safety net underneath a trapeze.

I watch the waves' low-slung, stealthy approach to the beach: suddenly, they are moving faster; grown upright, they swoop on the shore, as though whooping Red Indians, although the ragged hair they trail is white. They strike with an axe or knife, and make in the water the trajectory marks seen in comic books. The people who tussle with them manage buoyantly to survive.

From here, beyond the gulls roosted on the unbroken waves, the cove appears not much wider than my arm-span. The water has the raw smell of wet rust. I pedal on a one-wheel cycle, cranking back and forth to keep my balance, and idly play a little smooth jazz on the drums.

Sometimes I am taken up in a suddenly bulbous sea. The warm vague presence of the sky lifts me on its palm, to examine carefully such a fragile object, and then sets me all the way down. There are other swimmers further along who are exalted and relinquished in their turn.

I can make out on the hillside, as if through smeared glass, a row of thick-boled, widely peeled-open palm trees, among tiled roofs, at what must be a small park. The entangled blue smoke of the council's mowing machine is being combed out on the light.

Cars are shuttled back and forth as readily as abacus beads along the kinked wire of the shoreline road. There are big blocks of flats, like Bakelite wireless sets, on the cliff-tops, above the leaping-up white poodles of foam.

And now, as if while I were eating humid, salty rice, there had been coolly slipped into my mouth a sliver of crisp watermelon, I taste very distinctly for a moment the wet smell of new-mown grass that has come out to me on the air.

Tamarama Beach, Sydney

Impromptus

The motorcycle juggler
lies down in the road, beneath the vast monuments
of a cemetery
in the constellation of Orion.

*

Estuarine morning. The magpie's
alto speculations.
A woman plaits her hair
with its connivance.

*

The light in the corridor, taut as sunburn.
Grit on the lino at the beach house.
'All we need is some rain,' and the rain comes
and in lamplight hangs its golden combs.

*

The night is the storm's
and the Earth is
as the axe
owns the woodblock.

*

It can't be bad, polishing the glasses
before the big windows of the hotel
at Ballachulish. You will glimpse there at times the sunlit
uplands of an adjacent world.

*

In the bus, white neck,
black hair. Light has paused
on its endless journey.

*

Into the room, a breeze,
the pure note
on the ocean's single string.

*

Sunset, bushfire haze—
the city buildings are wrapped
in orange cellophane.

Among the Mountains of Guangxi Province in Southern China

I had been wading for a long while in the sands of the world
and was buffeted by its fiery winds,
then I found myself carried on a bamboo raft (I am speaking literally now),
poled by a boatman down the Li River.

A guest in Beijing at the Academy of Arts,
brought to the countryside,
I'd wandered out alone. A sheen on the night and across the ranks of water,
and close mountains that joined moonlit earth and sky.

When I saw the landscape around Guilin city
and realized it was still as the painter Xi Dao had known it,
in the Tang period, I felt suddenly exalted,
as though I were riding in the saddle of a cloud.

The mountains' outlines were crowded one behind another
and seemed a wild loosening of the brush,
a switchback scrubbing, rounded or angular,
until the last fibres of the ink had been used up, again and again.

Those narrow blue mountains make endless configurations.
They are by far the main crop the province bears.
Zhuang Zhou said that a twisted tree is not useful
and so it can survive for a thousand years.

A lead star plunged behind the mountains
as if the galaxy were crumbling more quickly than them.
How to convey the strangeness of this region?
I thought of migrating whales that break together, almost upright, out
of the sea.

That suggests their power, but not their stillness.
Some mountains reminded me of tall-hatted mushrooms,
some of veiled women, among a laden caravan, but all had a corroded
edging of trees.
We drifted by a few other rafts and their lanterns.

At times I saw rhinoceros horns, or a blackened cathedral,
at times the beauty of a carnivore's jawbone.
One place was as dramatic as a vertical wind-sock.
There was a broken palace in a fog-bound wilderness.

The next day we travelled to the village of Xin Ping
and found there drabness and squalor, a terrible indifference and
listlessness.
Worst of all, the poverty in people's faces,
the smallness of those lives. Everything was the colour of dust and
of smoke.

How can they not be embittered, and millions with them?
They see the comfort of cities, each night, on the communal television,
just hours off, and behind a stone door.
Earth could not bear the waste, were they all to have a fraction of what
they know.

We, who'd alighted there for a few days,
could love nature because of its indifference, and found our freedom
in that.

To do so, one must be secure. The same types of mountains were at
 Xin Ping
but I saw in them the sadness of eternal things.

Valedictory

I have come to an age where youth itself seems a virtue,
as beauty is, or wit. Her face was spotted
and her eyes were scared. She has renewed for me the phrase
'of tender years'. Tenderness flourished, when we spoke,
as it can on a tree that's been lopped away.
I went by train along the valley of the Elbe,
travelling like Janus with my mind on her. I am one who is disposed
to believe grace of the body is a state of the soul,
and have been misled before. I have also been persuaded it is immoral
to encourage those much younger than ourselves
to offer up the unripe fibres of their heart. So I wandered in Prague,
among the human plague; the bridge was in darkness
and the crowds were restless and dark. The last question she had asked of me
for her tape-recorder was, 'What is the question
you ask yourself?' I said, too easily, 'I have no questions,
if that means I imagine there can really be answers. I am not one of those
who believe that the world has gone astray.'
She looked at me with anxiety and with pity,
and wanted to talk. Therefore, young woman, I am travelling away from you.
(Also, I was urged by the driver to hurry.)
Now, I have the trams of Prague, the cobblestones, the dolls' houses
in pastel tones, pressed as it were out of jointed cardboard. On the way,
we came around the elbow and down the long forearm
of the river, which was narrow there and clothed
in a crinkled white sleeve. High up, like storm clouds, there were rock-faces,
and beneath these the terraces of pale-blue pines,
their branches shredded, down-trailing, each abashed as a retriever's tail.

In the tight valley floor, mustard-coloured flowers trickled through the grasses,
while close to the carriage window, the dark, twisted columns
were midges that fed on sunlight.
And I was struck, it seemed, with guilt, by the slow tolling
of a double-headed paddle, from a canoe, as we came by.
In Berlin, I'd had to ask
a question, myself, of a young woman, seeking directions
in the Hauptbanhoff. I chose, as one is inclined to on such occasions,
the most pleasant-looking person there.
She was standing in profile, and when she turned,
had a blind eye that was entirely silver,
like foil. I looked into this with a start, and of course
she was embarrassed, and I was embarrassed. But she was kind.
She did not deny or skimp her knowledge; but rather, carefully enunciating,
explained to me twice the way I should go.
Later, in the Pergamon, I found myself arrived before the famous bust
of Nefertiti, with her vacant eye, never restored—a choice
that it seems perfects her perfection—the queen of the slender throat,
who feels, you believe, the breeze on board an imperial ship,
as she is being carried upon swift oars. Dear girl
in Berlin, I wanted to praise your beauty, until you were as proud
as a sunflower on a bright day,
as drums, as a figurehead, as a shield, and an anthem.
Rilke has warned the artist
not to make himself ridiculous, in his years of recognition,
in his later years, through the undignified pursuit of younger women,
as he saw Rodin had done; causing pain and confusion, casting aside
with insufficient loyalty or care.
So many marvellous beings, whom we will never meet,
unless there is another life, or other lives.
This is what Whitman wished to believe—that we go on and on
along an open road, barefooted through the stars,
greeting others, with a clasp of them to ourselves. Hard to bear,

that we are shown these people who are like visions,
and yet never anything comes of it but that.
Such riches, which produce such poverty.

The School of Venice
for Michael and Kathrin Hulse

The Grand Canal can seem a swan
with its throat stretched out, when it is drawn
on the map. A creature that makes such opulent enquiry
could be the emblem of this city
and of its art.

The canal is a light green jade upon the chart,
as so often
it is in life. Or it's found amongst the finely-crazed porcelain
of an old, snapped-off medallion—
lanes and alleys
and equally profuse the waterways.
This swan, with neck unfurled,
has shown the enterprise of Zeus, in its seduction
of all the world.

Abundance through an ardent compensation
for natural lack is what
the city means. Although some have thought
locale is all we're taught,
I am inclined for once to be more Nietzschean.
Venice created Bellini
out of a particular paucity—
you find
finely limned

behind his Madonnas' resignation
perspectives of deprivation
in those blue earliest landscapes, which open out of smallness so
    spaciously.

In the same way,
the few, secretive Venetian gardens
provoked a memory of woods and mountains
for the young Titian—'perhaps the first painter to show a love
of particular mountains', in his case of
those types
which can be seen from his birthplace in the Dolomites;
and similarly with the perfect groves,
amid all their stroked leaves,
in his rhythmic idylls
and satin Bacchanals.
This tight city
produced out of insubordinance the immensities of Veronese;
while insouciant Tiepolo,
whom we rightly view from below,
gawping, made escape
upwards from restriction—we levitate
among the soles
of feet, calves, elbows, palms rested on air, the elbows of pinions,
blown hemlines, plump chins,
clouds like flung-off ermine stoles,
somersaulting *putti*
above a trampoline, and a view of a charger's hooves and belly.
His solution
was the one they would take up in Manhattan.

Turner's response to Venice, though, is too insubstantial,
too formless and 'spiritual';

he painted the city romantically,
isolating one attribute, what we see,
making it a vision. Venice isn't a dream,
or something made out of 'tinctured steam'.
Whatever might
its atmosphere has, the place is of stone as much as light.
(With bees, it's been found, only that is seen which has the brightness of
    jewels,
yet a swarm reels
off the reality of walls.
One's narrowed attention, out of incapacity, or thought,
doesn't negate
the world, whose nature remains inviolate.)

Still, the light of Venice is the essence of light,
a seething, powdery,
sifted light, especially
of a late afternoon. Then, it can seem that pink and white rose petals
    are strewn
over the city, that a whole mountain
of petals, blown on,
has whirled down
into the lagoon; and the petal-soaked water slaps
at St Mark's steps
and keeps on with its feathery
short movements, as if becoming a greenish honey.
(We were waiting with petals at our feet
for a motor-boat
to take us to the cemetery,
to an island of blackly wrapped cypresses, like Böcklin's 'Isle of the Dead',
but walled and elongated, where there is buried
E.P.)

This city was great when the Antipodes
were still undiscovered
by Europe. It has sung before it dies;
it is retired.
Nothing is being painted there or said
of merit now, as James Morris decades since claimed, and one soon believes.
Venice is a diet of pastries.
Ruskin's stone
resounds to a schoolgirl excursion, each on her mobile phone.
Two umbrellas wide, most *calle*
are lined with small shops, like bright cabinets—it is sideshow alley,
a fairground without ferris wheel,
a place of knick-knack and bauble,
a sticky light
to catch the world's shoppers, its overloaded freight.
Only very late
of an evening can we guess at the animus of other times:
along passageways,
unfolding emptily before us, there are footfalls like Harry Lime's
or the Doge's
agents, but no-one's in sight,
just a shadow, sucked about
a corner. And in the farthest reaches, where a lane becomes almost a tunnel,
beneath a slippery stone lip, the water's sinister as petrol.

The *palazzi* are dying on their feet, seen to be gangrenous at low tides,
although grandeur subsides
grandly. Their façades have minaret-shaped windows, lattice-work in stone,
small fenestrations in a four-leafed clover design,
great plinths for steps and sills,
columns, and decorative metal grilles.
They are always veiled by shutters
and in subdued colours:

terracotta, bone,
rust, or tan; occasionally a borsch, a blue-grey,
a lightest green.

Too eccentric a place to want to stay:
it was spring but the only bloom
was in buckets, or arranged in one's room.
Nowhere here
were there mountains in the end of a street, at the end of the day.
Yet, something not found elsewhere,
nor hoped for—that one could be ravished by decay.

II

Forgive this tourist's impression,
but Venice ought not to be an abstraction,
a word only; rather, it is water and stone, and a time, and a person.
I was in Venice for your wedding, with to follow
lunch at Torcello,
another island, where you had us go
by speedboat. It was quiet and dry there, mainly in ruins,
the trees like brambles. We were led to a garden's
fine gravel, of an amber afternoon. This restaurant formerly
a wooden farmhouse. But what we first must see,
you told us, was the Byzantine interior
of Santa Maria dell' Assunta,
from about 600, its marvelous
mosaics, a short way off. I became at once preoccupied with the fear
and obsequiousness
that had gathered there
for so long; it was probably because of the Virgin's stare,
remote and superior,
within freezing stone.

That place was as cold as God's love. I tried to imagine their religion:
icy Hell on one cheek, on the other
the effervescent thin light of a steamy Heaven…
Whereas, the love
of feeling oneself alive,
a confident, sure
grasp of the world, and the triumph of pleasure,
are, according to Berenson,
in his book, what we owe the Venetian
school of art. Employees of the Church, he praises in them their happy
     treason.
That day, sun shone
and the cold that could take your face off the bone
was left behind. Flowers, for which men work
for their own sake,
had appeared again, in the garden
where we were seated, for the best of cuisines, the Italian.

III

Here in Rome, resident
for a while, I make this wedding present,
and remember unexpectedly a Chekhov story,
called rather daringly
'A Boring Story'.
You most likely will know it—a young woman
visits an aged professor,
her guardian, whose illness means he can't survive much longer,
and asks him in desperation,
and in the Russian way, to give
her advice, how she's to live.
'Help me!' she sobs. 'You are my father,
the only one in whom I have faith, you are clever,

educated, you
have lived so long. What am I to do
with myself?' (She has wanted to be an actress
but in her distress
tells him she is a failure
at that: no talent.) 'Which way do I go?'
He has to say, 'Upon my word, Katya,
I do not know.'
But he implores her,
all the same, 'Let us have lunch, Katya dear'; which provokes her disdain
and she leaves. And he is sure
there won't be time to see her again.
'Farewell, my treasure…'
How wise a man
Chekhov was. Perhaps unknown
to his character,
'Let us have lunch' is a serious rejoinder.
This is a toast I ought to have made
at your table, for us, and for everyone
(I would want it taken
in its wide
implication).
I don't mean we should do so intemperately,
except perhaps occasionally,
and of course it is not enough of an answer
(thinking of Venice, and of Italy,
with their culture
diminuendo), as Chekhov knew. Through any book
of his, there is another
piece of advice, repeatedly (it is in his letters and his life)—that we
    should work
unselfishly.
Some complain

of such talk, that the air of the Enlightenment is too thin.
This is hardly our choice, or of our doing. Still, here where finally
   we belong,
the lungs grow strong;
and Enlightenment means that something is done
about certain of God's more intricate design.
(You will have guessed that I am feeling deluged by religion
in this city. Too many churches visited;
high camp, practically
all, though I've admired
Santa Cecilia, and Santa Maria in Trastevere…)
Chekhov came to Rome
not long before he would die, on returning home,
at forty-four. In the Vatican
he watched a procession with a friend, and that man
said, 'What splendour…
How would you describe this?' Chekhov's answer:
'A long line of silly monks dragged tediously by.'
What I wanted to say
is, Don't you think the Enlightenment could have had an origin,
or have found a way-station
on its way from Greece,
in the real light
of Venice
and of Tuscany,
which are evoked and dwelt on in those places' art?
It descended through Claude, and many another,
who kindled their brushes in its fire,
and took it hence,
first of all to France.
Anyway, I can see,
clearly as on that trestle, the shuffling of leaf-shadow and wine
before each one

of our small party, met again,
from the world, in Europe.
Our glasses are raised another time, as though each of us held a peony
or tulip.

Thinking of Harriet

Years back, come to Japan, my step-daughter,
in our fifth-floor apartment, made a bound
from off the matting, and as she landed
the entire building shook. Her eyes were round.

The Creek

The slow effervescence of wind-lifted rain
on knuckle and cheekbone
a sweet
occasional prickling
that is met while I walk above the creek, having come down a lane
and out to the back
of the long yards at the edge of town
a fragile assault
in the steamy afternoon.

The red earth's compacted in the high creek bank
baked tight
and a rope swing is looped
among the trees rising from beneath here that are inclined
through the element
of ointment.
These tapering swamp oaks are each drawn overhead

like a splinter that's festered.
The grass on top of the bank leads back to the plank
palisades
above one of which there perches a folded and dove-breasted
blue smoke
nested in the triple-ply of summer air.

And the green fretwork of a *Monstera deliciosa* plant
against the palings
is Matissean
in this unstylish small town, in the sleeping quarters
of the hinterland—
it seems the one reminder of *luxe, calme et volupté*
when our inheritance
is an Irish Sunday.

Grey weather between the high-grown, thickly gathered trees, the lean
sparse-leaved eucalyptus poles,
parsley-
shelved, but with frail
grey-green leaves, and down the slope the kettle-black
lower boles
among which the water's glimpsed—the secret creek in khaki that beats
like a vein at the throat
of someone
who's lying hidden.
Here from an open place I once saw a slick naked black snake
quick
switchback swimming
through all of its two metres
along the creek, encompassing
it in swathes—a wound-up and then let-go, fast
mechanical progression

into the dark
entangled mud; the crab
legs akimbo
of the black mangroves at the water's low margin.

But today there is only the egret's ancient Egyptian
délicatesse, its foot
professed
in profile on the bevel
of sand-
tipped shore. With its mosquito-fine
placement
I see it again
accomplish
a step, towards the swirl
of rain or of a fish.

The egret is shapely and tapering as an amulet
or a slim gourd
it's compact
as though smoothed between the hands
the neck
is kinked and finely drawn-out, which suggests a loose
length of vine
sharply trimmed-off, and it is seemingly ineffectual,
pensive.
One can imagine
as its claim that to pick the excess
from small life
is an honorable
scheme. It steps out of the stillness and stands
still again
and blue

like backyard smoke,
among the aimless insects of the sunlit rain.

Joan Eardley in Catterline

The black-faced sheep
are tilted in the storm-light and they face the black-faced
North Sea
from the long decline

of their swollen
pasture. Over all of this, the same
inertia. The weeds and fence posts come down and hang
above the lane

and we pass beneath
a bank that oozes like a luminous, wrung-out kitchen cloth. The
barn
opens on a corner
its tunnel

directly out of the gravel
kerb. We slide
by in a car, swishing over mashed cow manure and sliding water.
Joan Eardley
came here,
following the reports
on the news, to a place with the worst of
weather, to a cove
that in itself is as rough as the jaws of a wrench.
The tight cottages
are fastened to each other and to the headlands

of tight grass; one row on either. Otherwise, there is a pub.

She brought her cancer,
stepped down
into the rattling edges of the bay, with an easel
of lead pipes, it must have been. The storms here

are an opened furnace door
of wind and snow. She stood in the sea,
the water ahead
higher than her painting board,

as we knew
from Aberdeen's quiet gallery. The sea fell like a weir,
corrugated in black and white; the sky was seasick, a greenish-grey;
the grey sea
greasy as stone, and its foam

ruinous yellow, from the churned-up
shallow floor. Or else,
there was the release, the transformation, of peach blossom
on thickly-packed black sticks. She broke open

the paint, wound it together, squalled her graffiti
along the water's façade, scoured
with blunt spines, adjusted everything under a clunky spanner,
undid
at the slice of a trowel,
dug her fingernails in, engrossed. Her subject,
death's approach,
become subject
to her.

Or she turned inland, into the passages of the sun—
to that over-ripe
pecked fruit,
which at other times seemed a sniveling, dangled

mucous, and at times had the liquid redness
of an organ
squashed into a jar. The sun, among
the broken panes

of the sticks
and the long grassy skeins,
waning,
was also painted as her own,

with an urgency occluding distance and time. Bits of straw and rope,
grass seeds and bent nails, were caught up,
among paint
that she lived in like the mud. Joan Eardley in Catterline at home.

I think of someone great,
of Dōgen, in his death poem. 'For fifty years I have hung
the sky with stars; and now I leap through.—
What shattering!'

Poem

In the night, a guttering that overflows onto concrete
makes the sound of a big dog at its drinking bowl.
From where I am lying I can see through slanted
blinds the rain settle on the red fur of the
motel sign. Later, getting up, I open the blinds
a span and there is a gull banking on the
coagulated moonlight.

Minima

The beautiful in nature
is that which symbolizes for us
a desirable state of being.

Reality can't be something
projected by our minds, since mind
is unable to affect it.

Apollo rides on
the shoulders of Dionysus—
otherwise is repugnant.

To be absorbed
in something is to have gone beyond
concern with happiness.

Our compulsions and motives
are as abstruse to us
as they are to other people.

The sense of quiddity
is mysticism
for materialists.

I have faith
that there is no such personage
as God would be.

We've come to fear science
because it brings bad news.
It is our only friend.

What is the neutral ground
we stand upon
when making our free choice?

Darwin shows us marvellous things;
the development of life, and of the mind,
occur entirely by accident.
(Possibilities need not be fulfilled.)

People who don't like
one's ideas often seem to think
that refutes them.

The only apology
for existence is
that it's so various.

Even if random,
a genetic mutation is
an imposition.

We 'affirm life'
because we must, but not
with all our heart.

Good is the conclusion
that we draw from evil.

Those who devalue pleasure
for themselves are likely to undervalue
pain for others.

Moral pleasure is reassurance
about human beings.
It is this we find so moving
in a work of art.

The senses can mislead us,
it is true, when we rely on
only one of them.

What we love about nature
is its unresponsiveness—
it is precisely
that it doesn't 'care or know'.

The sensory pleasures of the world
aren't merely transitory,
as the other-worldly claim,
but are constantly
renewed and refreshed for us.

Unselfishness has often
a selfish motive—
accolade (not least one's own).

We feel nature act in us, and think
we originated the impulse,
but all our identification
comes after the event.

Épater les bourgeois? Certainly,
but there is another complacency one mustn't
overlook: *Épater les avant-gardistes.*

This weed only survives
because it is so weak. Grasp it
anywhere and it breaks above the root.

Sanssouci

Frederick the Great's
summer palace, a rococo-style
pavilion, with windows
that could make
a glass house,
is the yellow
of Hollandaise sauce
and has egg-white detail.

It arises, encrusted with sculptural
gestures, on a billow
at the edge of a great park. Below
the blazing gravel

of its forecourt, there is laid out
what has been the project
of his heirs, also—

the gardens. These are loose,
English, pluralist,
and proliferate
among copse and alcove,
gathering mist
in any niche or hollow
toward dusk. They've
shaggy hedges and rank-
looking northern trees
by Cranach,
are not at all Platonist.

Frederick came here
if he wished to be alone,
with just a hundred servants,
and played the flute, in thigh boots,
before banks of candlelight,
or walked the grounds with Voltaire.

He gave shelter, from Catholic
and Protestant, to La Mettrie,
who had pointed out
man is a machine of meat
driven by appetite
(there was a comparison made also
with a plant)—i.e.,
we are subject
to cause and effect.
Frederick composed his eulogy.

The Prince liked homosexual jokes
and saw his wife once a year
at a state occasion.
His nephew was his heir.
He wrote an Anti-Machiavel
and had four horses shot
from under him in battle.
He was a hero to Napoleon.

Although a *philosophe*
he built an army
of those who had no say
and took them
into hand-to-hand slaughter,
to break upon his hip
the sway
of Austria-Hungary.
As Engels used to quip,
History fulfils her purposes—
her potential—by wading
over stacks of corpses.

The clear-eyed Greeks
were in Frederick's thoughts
at Sanssouci,
as seen by the statuary
he'd planted
at each of the circuses
along the main graveled courses
and in alcoves
off the mazed pathways.
(At major junctions, as well,
there are fountains, each a simple

pool, with its tall
water like an ostrich feather.)

The gods and heroes here
are shown
at what they've always done,
which is bestir
trouble. Life
as the Greeks knew
is mischief. To interfere
is the way of Nature.
Aphrodite, though
she turns her face away
and covers breast
and pubis, is inflammatory
just because
of that modesty.
Beside her are displayed,
along with wheelbarrow and spade,
the usual abductions, rapes
and punishments,
in radiant nudity.

In one arbour
Hercules crumbles the spine
of Antaeus, who is embraced
about the waist, and hung
off the ground, a leg thrown
back, a toe feebly
reaching, to plug in
to the Earth.
Cinch of his girth
by half, his swollen scream

soundless, the extruded tongue
like a spear thrust
from behind, out of his mouth.
Undermined, the whole building
is coming down.

For those sauntering
of a late afternoon, the trees
and shrubberies
make a backdrop
to this scene, and are laden
with leaves, as a window
with blown rain. You see,
drawn near, in the level
glare, the foliage
is like tongues,
and it is these that the sun
lays its wafer upon.

Classifying the Animals

There are those that in the distance seem a swarm of gnats
those that with their barking try to rally us in a campaign against the stars
those that torment their prey
those that follow both sides of an argument
those that have broken a precious vase
those that can only be painted with a one-haired brush
those whose tongues light candles on the fingers of our hands
those that curl their tails
those that refute the Argument from Design, such as bedbugs and liver fluke
stupid ones, who lie still for a while and then run
those whose being is clenched, as though a knot in a frozen rope

mosquitoes
crocodiles
the good-natured beetles
those such as frogs and snails that sit in meditation
humans, born unable to stand
those that are fit to be emblazoned on a flag
those that should exist—unicorns and mermaids
unacceptable ones, unless we can make a great rational effort
those that cause people to smile—ladybirds, etc.
those that stir in us an erotic feeling
those that are easily broken and yet their kind continues to exist
those that one would like to be—the centaur, the phoenix.

Ekphrasis

'Manhunt Near My Home' by Irvine Homer, 1959
for Tom Carment

The artist was a farm labourer
in what he called 'jam tin country'
and himself a captive
when he painted the escapee.

Nineteen fifty-nine, Emu Plains—
there met on a prison farm,
where they were held for car theft,
the 'youths' Simmonds and Newcombe,

who broke out. One was caught
in days. This picture reminds
of how at fourteen I admired
that 'Houdini', Kevin Simmonds.

Each day for weeks, the largest
manhunt in our history,
and yet the wireless told us
that again he'd slipped away,

despite 500 police,
with submachine-guns and flares
and a helicopter, and despite
the 300 volunteers.

For all the legends, rebellion
is light in our inheritance.
What outraged the populace
was in fact a mischance—

Surprised, in making the escape,
one of them gave a smack
to a guard, with a baseball bat,
and caused his skull to crack.

Something they had often seen
in a Saturday picture show,
but the sort of weight to apply
was difficult to know.

There are, I realize now,
further victims in such a crime.
They made him 'comfortable'
with a blanket—waste of time.

The police look to their own
and moved like a bushfire;

brought back Ray Kelly, inspector,
who'd wanted to retire;

his style, an axe's bite;
the professed killer of three men;
in trench coat, felt hat, iced
spectacles; temper worn thin.

So Newcombe was caught. Later,
they found what Simmonds would do
was break into cars and listen
to the police radio.

He flickered through ragged suburbs,
eluding the blades of torches,
dissolved in misty streetlight
(food sometimes on back porches).

After school, with my bike, I had
the newspaper delivery
for a country town; and each day
paused, to follow this story

in different papers. Then pedalled
at twilight about the town
on gravel streets and grass verges;
the rolled newspapers thrown

into the yards I pretended
were sticks of dynamite
that would scare off the bloodhounds
and put the police to flight.

A rebel with cause—the suburbs.
Ahead of the sixties, his hair
like Elvis. I admired him
more than any pop star.

And here he is in this picture,
near Newcastle, New South Wales,
a hundred miles from Sydney,
in a culvert as light fails.

Along the base, a dirt road,
at a see-saw's tilt, and under
this is where he's hidden;
above, two policemen linger.

To the left, the road turns in,
around a black, cairn-shaped hill;
from the right, a forest headland;
between a skewed triangle

of orange grass, with wind-break trees.
Across this clearing, minutely,
the police disperse, clothes-peg shapes;
or like ants, you'd have to say.

Then purple forest, in long pleats
of cold slag, laid transversely;
light on undulant edges of
elided gullies. Poignantly,

a thin straight line of powdered smoke's
leaving. Lawrence called reptilian

the ancient stillness of the bush.
A dog; a coughing policeman.

And higher still, dark promontories
and a bleached ocean appear,
out of the Northern Renaissance,
by Altdorfer or Patenier.

An electric sunset: plum blue
to one side, with stacked thunder;
a new world in the other half,
its rosy and golden moisture.—

Coral canyons and crests, a lit
engorgement; the confluence
of labile traceries;
a strawberry deliquescence;

some honeyed Apocalypse;
magnolias' scalloped ivory;
the bruised limbs of seraphim;
an orchidean Arcady;

as if in divine armada
Deity called on us at home
wanting to anoint the Earth,
our estrangement overcome.

This to balance Simmonds, taken
in a swamp, at twenty-four;
now open-faced, brave, resourceful,
but he would race no more.

Vengefully they'd seal away
all that he might have been.
Laying hands on him for photos,
Ray Kelly, brought to the scene.

Is that sunset meant to show
a heaven he'll never win
Not an angel with its trumpet
nor a scroll has been painted in.

Is it to show us 'the lilies
…on the banks of Italy';
that there's no separation
between beauty and cruelty?

The painter, self-taught, bed-ridden;
the brushes tied to his wrists;
both legs had been amputated
because of spondylitis.

Simmonds was put into Grafton,
the worst-reputed prison;
I saw the law as blood-stained
that well knew what would happen—

I'd heard of the 'Reception.'
In a few years, hanged himself;
grown tired of being beaten,
the only way to get relief.

I often used to imagine
there'd been a chance for him,

that a generous woman beckoned
as in a Hitchcock film—

Like Psyche, at the prow of time
that figure comes to stand
within the window's bay, a wand
of candlelight in her hand.

Impromptus

Rain towards morning...
A last house above the shore
where I used to go with my heart
knocking at the door.

'Butter in the corners
of your bread,'
grandfather advised,
a house-painter by trade.

A woman sponges
her side, one arm resting on
a cloud.
The magpie's song.

She scoops up her dog
(ours is uncouth),
an armful of soap
off a bubble bath.

In the crisp night
of a country town, as I amble

about, someone says, 'Have you had your medicine yet?
Dinner's on the table.'

All the wet day, lights burn
at the house opposite,
and gulls stand
in puddles about the lawn.

An owl floats over,
a balloon, so quiet,
its breast puffed full
of moonlight.

All day, the windows' grey weather,
above the Sound,
and waters file by
through the turnstiles, all day.

A cyclist in the country night, in a light
mist. His light
disappears in hollows for a while,
and then he comes on, with sprocket clanking.

In a new suburb, in light rain,
at the road's verge treading its line
with the stateliness of a tightrope walker,
concentrating, the diesel roller.

So poor, we boiled all
our eggs for the week together.
Mum scraped butter off its wrapping paper.
We hid the ketchup sandwiches when at school.

An old man's laconics
about weather he'd known
at a slant the bull's
testicles.

On the small-town barber shop floor
snippings of black hair;
they're exploded ideograms.
Futurism in Japan.

A waiting room, near midnight.
His lips are moving quietly,
who's either semi-literate
or reading poetry.

A Wing Beat

In some last inventory, I'll have lost a season,
through the occlusion
of summer by another hemisphere.
Going there,
the winter will toll twice
across the year. The leaves of ice
are manuscript
shelved on the air, and sift
fine as paper-cuts along the wind. I will go
to crippled snow
that rolls through crossings in its wheelchair, before the headlights
of early nights.
How glorious summer is to them
who have caught just a glimpse of its billowing hem.
'Fifty springs are little room,' an authority

in loss warns, but statistically
I can expect to own
ten summers, before the heights of blue close down.
Although I've gone
northwards, I will cross the lawn
at home—the trees and yard in bloom—
in the mirror in an empty room.

The Sea-Wall
(after paintings by Ted Hillyer)

The headland has been raided,
eaten, broken away,
a carcass that hyenas
have found. It is the quarry

for the wall, drawn from it,
a rough intestine of stone;
this jumble of shapes like
DNA or protein.

Among them, a cement lane
goes nowhere, to carry
with bold gesture to sea
just the track of a railway

that built it (now rust flakes
and the sleepers' imprint).
Added each side, more recent,
are great blocks of cement.

The purpose the wall served
has been lost, apart from
that of swimmers and paddlers,
now that ships never come.

On the wall, looking back past
broken edge and sharp angle,
the line of the headland
holds its ravaged blue metal.

I have seen the wall at dawn
from its headland, silhouette
of a stamen, weighed with seed,
among the sea's milky-white.

The people come here early
to sit on flat roof-tops
in a street of skewed pueblos,
which they drape with bright stripes.

And here they pluck the garden
of the sea, in its alcoves,
or snorkel above rocks,
and laugh when ocean shoves

heavily (a whale with spume)
the outer curve. They cover

just eyes and genitals,
organs of too much pleasure.

Behind them, soap flakes sprinkled;
then higher, along the sea,

soap-powder; and then lathered
clouds, a whole bright laundry.

Children ride their bikes here,
and men gut fish they've caught;
a woman on the ocean
has a red towel drawn straight

behind her, and levers it
slowly back and forth; her breasts
solemnly eye those passing.
The finest sea-spray floats

in the hair on forearms, on
a girl's lip; feet are slapped
through puddles; in chevrons
of shade, picnics unpacked.

The sea's striped purple, blue-green,
chrome. Nearby, an idle yacht,
a black dog, framed by its sail,
on a pedestal, alert.

Slightly curved, as fishing rods
are, the wall unfailingly
sprouts its riffled fine bristles
on the days that are holy.

Impromptus

My grandmother, an Anderson,
was speaking of me, I could have sworn,
when she told my sister
'Kohlrabi for dinner.'

Who stole the cripple's ukulele
or stole the cripple away?
I used to fear for him, playing underfoot
in the halls of the railway.

In my dream, I was leaned far out
among the cordage
of a yawl, in the morning
of the world.

'Just half a loaf, Arthur.'
On his bike
he drifts into the night, and seems a yacht,
a white shadow passing.

When we come to reminisce,
a silver tear
falls from us both
among the cutlery.

Wading in ferns, waist deep
at twilight. On the horizon
a tanker barely moves, and the clouds
are translucent as pearls.

Dust and twigs, leaves,
membranous water;
a first sunlit passage
the bee swarm of day.

Along the tight poles of eucalypts,
across their vanished height,
making them seem stage curtains with deep pleats
the night train's bare spotlight.

The Latter Days

I sit on the porch in darkness
and imagine I have been assigned to watch here on my own.
At 3 o'clock everyone is sleeping,
no distant drone
of a car now, nor bird chirping.
Downhill, there was wiped from the town
the last house-lights, as if they were moisture.
The main street goes on
beyond its lamps, which seem pinches of salt, and becomes out in the landscape
    a javelin thrown.

There is an engorged moon
and all the shattered stars, and there's one sullen light across the valley—
a farmhouse, on its mountain,
beneath the folded plumage of the sky.
The range there
is crumpled, as the blanket is
I have drawn about me. I am reminded by that blood-shot glare
I was tonight in Hades,

or believed so. I went down through a gate in the marshland,
in a reek of sulphur,
and passed below what must have been a lintel,
into thin flavourless metal air.
Then I realized that the souls in Hades
cannot change, since they've been judged,
and I understood, too late, there was no point in seeking
my father's bitter face among the Shades.

Yet I must go on.
It was not for revenge—there is only grief.
Although I have grown old
this is an ageless wound.
The regret is for his chances, all lost in dissipation. That is as difficult
as always, and growing older, it would seem,
has served no purpose at all.
I thought I came there through a forest, where the trees were howling like dogs.
Thick as the leaves of an endless autumn
that I had trod
in the wilderness, on the river bank
were the dead,
swept together, wearied,
who waited for a ferry, which would mean their journey was almost ended.
Somehow I stepped across the Stygian water,
and Pluto sat in the plain, as though a crag upreared.
Proserpine lay along his side,
under a pall of steamy darkness.
They were draped in cerements, from their lustreless crowns to the ground,
and I could not see her beauty,
for which she was snatched away
while gathering flowers in the meadows of Enna.
The tremulous souls on the bare plains behind her
were as numerous as grass might have been.

Then my father appeared
on a single warp in the atmosphere
(while the hands of the dead fell upon me
in a feeble rain). And of course he was as he must always be—
he had no guilt, not even feigned,
no greeting for me. As in the nursing home,
I felt him demand, of earth and of the zenith, 'Get me out of here.'
Pitiful spirit,
born of an ill-featured star,
hollowed by thirst, he seemed to say, with all of his old extremity,
'There is no crime
I would not commit
to be born again, and take my chances on earth.'
Young men blame others, and old men themselves, except for him.
And his clamour was sealed away
in the human quicksand of the crowd.

For a while, they have their little dreams there
that show them they are sleeping.
But no one can live forever, not even the dead. They will fade.
It is suggested
in Virgil that only a few heroes ever reach
those shimmering light-filled uplands of the blest, Elysium.

Then I found I had got up and was leant against the railing,
to feel on my face the tender
incandescence of the dew.
There was a snarl
of lightning, where it threw itself along the horizon.
I brought a drink out
and saw, in passing, the piled-up cold woodash trickle
in the grate, as when a breeze,

memento mori,
stirs among the feathers of a guinea fowl.

The advantage of having sought an education
was Virgil as companion,
although, of course, he did not condescend
to walk with me. I had for a guide-book
what was made of him by Dryden,
in sufficient accuracy.
I knew what one must do: that in Hades you break off
the candelabra of a bough
from out of a misty tree; each flame
on this becomes gold-leaf, and you carry it before you
onto the wide steps
that lead steeply into darkness, welling from below.
The branch is for Proserpine, an offering,
its small light
to be planted in her shadow, although it will not flourish.

One time, we greeted our father as 'Mr Shellfish',
playing with a remark our mother had made.
He ignored us
except to point out that Horace found abhorrent
any violation of the ordinance of nature
such as was involved in calling him a crab.
He contended that his pension was meant for him,
who'd been infested with TB, while mired on a side-line
of the War. If our mother reminded him that it was self-inflicted,
and was exacerbated
continuously, he would retaliate by wounding us
with the porcelain claw
of his disdain.

I associate him always with the Latin authors. He seemed to believe
their language was his, to keep alive.
It was in him an exoneration. For such remarks as the one above,
when I came to understand it,
I would have carried him on my back,
out of his ruins.

I have a neighbour, along the hillside,
an old woman who loves to read.
She goes to bed early, and I imagine that when she is tired
she folds her glasses on the bedside stand
and then her arms, in the same way, on her punctured chest,
and is at rest. Now at dawn, this woman shouts
into the paddocks, and her dog shouts back. It tells her
to exult. She has her fulfilment.
What appears to be an armful of wattle is brought to us here
at daybreak and at nightfall,
lightly, without piety or desert—I see it being carried for me
from the rim of the world,
among the bushland's broken foliage.
And I had wondered, while wandering in the mazed ways of last night,
how I was to reach
the light again. Then I realized
that where I found myself, amid all the emphasis
on stasis,
can be seen through, as a delusion. It vanished from me, like eluding a
     theme
in the glissando of a violin.
Our imagination is something more dreadful than the truth,
although it is an essential affliction.
Take Deiphobus, who was called 'bashful'
in Dryden's rendering,
since he was beautiful, but his nose and ears had been sliced off,

and he knew it was Helen,
his wife, who had betrayed him, beside her first husband Menelaus.
(I suppose she felt
that she had beauty enough for them both.)
Such knowledge, it was conjectured,
meant he must live
for the extent of a horde of lifetimes, to be rid of animus.
In life, everything is insecure and arbitrary,
we've innumerable opportunities
for taking offence.
The only solution is not to be.
The dead exist for none but the living. If we pursue them
their souls smell in Hades. We turn away.
They are ashes to ashes and dust on the wind.

Ingres' Violin
(selected pencil drawings)

Self-portrait

Girl in a cafe

Heat haze

228

Southern England)

Girl in a train from Milan to Rome

Sam

Eucalyptus branches

Dale

Mother at 94

Scotland off the road

Ted the painter

Watsons Bay

Paddock in moonlight